Praise for *From Loving One to One Love*

From Loving One to One Love is one of the most accessible, relatable and illustrative books I've ever read about the teachings of special vs. holy relationships in *A Course in Miracles*. If you are truly ready to experience awakening, the fastest road is not through individual enlightenment as you might expect, but through the very relationships that challenge us the most. This book will help you get there. It will provide you with the inspiration, insight and motivation needed to repurpose your relationships as vehicles through which healing can be received by all. I love this book and wholeheartedly recommend it!

—Corinne Zupko, Ed.S., award-winning and
bestselling author of *From Anxiety To Love*

Dr. Bob Rosenthal's latest book, *From Loving One to One Love*, is a delightful exploration of using relationships to find inner freedom and awaken to Divine Love. . . . The importance of releasing the past through applied forgiveness is offered as a way of finding the mind's portal to holy relationship. Bob's therapist experiences and articulate examples shine Light on a most profound and adventurous pathway to Truth.

—David Hoffmeister, author,
This Moment Is Your Miracle

T0145954

From
Loving One
to
One Love

Transforming Relationships
through *A Course in Miracles*

ROBERT ROSENTHAL, M.D.

Published by Gildan Media LLC
aka G&D Media.
www.GandDmedia.com

FIRST EDITION: 2020

FIRST PAPERBACK EDITION: 2021

Front cover design by David Rheinhardt of Pyrographx

Interior design by Meghan Day Healey of Story Horse, LLC.

Library of Congress Cataloging-in-Publication Data is available upon request

ISBN: 978-1-7225-0540-0

10   9   8   7   6   5   4   3   2   1

For my wife and life partner, Emmanuelle,
who has taught me more about love and relationships
than I ever imagined possible. Thank you, love—for
everything! We walk the path to reawakening together.

And for Tamara Morgan, fellow co-president and
partner in guiding the Foundation for Inner Peace.
What a long, strange trip since we first met—proof that
the Holy Spirit sees the big picture and we do not.
I am grateful to you for joining me in
sharing the love of this holy relationship.
May it extend to include everyone.

Contents

Part One
Loving One: Relationships

Part Two
Grievance and Forgiveness

Part Three
One Love

Foreword

Dr. Robert Rosenthal and I were both present on June 26, 1976, at the home of Judy Skutch Whitson in the historic Beresford apartment building on Central Park West in New York City when the first printed editions of *A Course in Miracles* were handed out.

Neither of us could have known then the immense breadth and depth of the books we held in our hands. Nor could we have understood how these words would change our lives, our understanding of this world, the implications for mental health, and our appreciation for that Life which transcends the insanity of the ego's world—a world we are so often tempted to see before us.

The Course has quite rightly been called a "modern spiritual classic." It is indeed a masterpiece. The deeper we go into this transformational work, the deeper we see that this Course is taking us all the way Home. Most incredibly, the goal of this Course is enlightenment.

It is with joy that I offer my sincere appreciation of Dr. Bob Rosenthal's well written, clear, simple statement of the basic principles of *A Course in Miracles* and how we might directly apply these principles. He does so with humor, anecdotes, and insights arising from his practice as a psychiatrist. He provides a gentle exposé of the ego's longing for specialness and of a clear differentiation between "special love" as the ego would construct it to insights into "real love" as God shares His love with us through these incredible words of Jesus as found in the Course.

We don't have to do anything to earn God's love; and for the sake of our own happiness, all we need to do is to get out of our "not-self's" shadow so that we might then be illumined. All we have to do is to "be" the love that we already are, forgiving ourselves for having entertained the ego, and get on with "Loving Life, Loving God, and thus Loving all there is."

As Dr. Bob points out, we do not speak of "rising in love," rather do we "fall" in love; and falling often hurts, especially when sobriety sets in. Then, the impetuous and often unthinking ego "falls out" of love—ouch! How painful this can be. What we need quite simply is to engage in a process of "purification." As the Course tells us "Miracles are everyone's right, but purification is necessary first." Once we have responsibly removed the blocks to an awareness of love's presence, God's love can then pour forth onto all of life, all the time, without condition. The result is that we are happy, and being happy, the world around us somehow "miraculously" improves.

Perfect love does not exist in a fantasy world. That we'll leave for the movies. Perfect love does exist, however, within God's Kingdom and the Kingdom of Heaven is "within you,"—not the temporal body but the eternal mind. As the Course tells us in the first Chapter, *Only perfect love exists. If there is fear, it produces a state that does not exist.* Real love can be found only within our relationship with the Universe and within ourselves; we are a part of God. Ultimately, we see, there is no way to escape from God, from this One love so—we're better off taking God/Love into our full embrace.

> Lovingly, Jon Mundy,
> Ph.D., author of *Living A Course in Miracles*
> www.miraclesmagazine.org

Preface

Valentine's Day and the
Course of True Love

From Loving One to One Love is a book about transforming relationships. As of this writing, the book has been scheduled for release on February 14, 2020, Valentine's Day, a day dedicated to the celebration of romantic love—a day of flowers, hearts, chocolates, dinners out, and of course greeting cards to express to those we love how much we love them. Cupid's arrows fly thick and fast on this day—but for most, to no great effect. If you're yearning for that special someone who's managed to elude your oh-so-subtle attentions, it's unlikely your "Be my Valentine" card will have much impact. And if you're already a couple, then why wait for Valentine's Day to say "I love you"?

The holiday is iconic; its signature hearts have become a permanent fixture of our emoji-laden world. However, few are aware of the holiday's darker origins in the ancient Roman feast of Lupercalia, which was celebrated from

February 13–15. During this festival, drunken males would sacrifice a goat or a dog, skin the animal, and then use its hide to whip women, who lined up to receive such treatment in the belief it would make them more fertile. The men were naked—of course! There was also a lottery in which men could draw the names of eligible women to pair up with in what today would be called a random hookup. The holiday gets its name from the Roman emperor's execution on February 14 of two different individuals, both named Valentine. Both were martyred and later canonized by the church. In light of this lurid historical background, who could be blamed for having second thoughts about romantic love?

If you've bought this book on Valentine's Day, you might be hoping that it will reveal the secret to attracting your perfect partner or "soul mate"—or if you've already found that person, how to hold onto them. That would be a mistake. What this book *will* do is help you discover the true meaning of love so that you can find it in *all* of your relationships—your lover and partner, and also your family, friends, and acquaintances. That is the goal of the spiritual masterpiece *A Course in Miracles* (commonly referred to as "the Course"), and on its very first page the Course says this about love:

> *The course does not aim at teaching the meaning of love, for that is beyond what can be taught. It does aim, however, at removing the blocks to the awareness of love's presence, which is your natural inheritance.*[1]

*   *   *

According to the Course, love is natural. It is *inherent* in what you are. This means you don't have to *do* anything to obtain it. You *are* love and so is everyone else. *"Love, which created me, is what I am."* [2] At some deep level you already know this. That is why it does not need to be taught to you. But you have forgotten. And you will not remember love unless you remove the obstacles that block you from it. It is this unblocking process that the Course calls *forgiveness*.

In the pages that follow, I will offer a radical repurposing of your understanding of relationships. No longer will you view them as arrangements made between you and one or more special individuals. Rather, you will learn how all of your relationships can shine in the reflection of the One Love from which we were all created, namely, the Love of God. To the extent that you're willing to embrace that goal your relationships will transform, and they will do so in ways that may seem miraculous because they can't be explained or understood rationally. They transform not because of what you do, but because of what we are— Love—and your remembrance of that truth. This is the path of *A Course in Miracles*.

Author's Notes

This book is the second in a series titled The Principles of *A Course in Miracles*. In the first book, *From Never-Mind to Ever-Mind: Transforming the Self to Embrace Miracles*, I distilled down the most fundamental teachings of the Course and presented them in a straightforward, understandable and hopefully enjoyable manner. Needless to say, you will get more out of the series if you read the books in order as they were intended.

* * *

The Course uses many words associated with conventional Christianity, words like "sin," "salvation," "Christ," and "Atonement." In the first book of this series, I chose not to use these words out of concern that some readers unfamiliar with the Course might be put off by them. In this book I will be using them. If you find yourself triggered as a result of old church and Sunday-school associations, remember that the Course's terminology may indeed echo that of conventional Christianity, but only because it attempts to reinterpret it and make its words congruent with Jesus's powerful message of love.

All quotes from the Course are in italics. All other quotes are not. Course quotes are annotated to a reference key that you will find at the end of the book.

The Course was scribed during the 1960s, well before the need for gender-neutral pronouns was recognized. It uses the patriarchal form of language found in the Bible because its goal is to realign the teachings of Jesus with their original meaning, which has unfortunately been distorted throughout much of the Bible. Therefore phrases like "Son of God" and "your brothers" occur frequently.

Because this is a book about *A Course in Miracles*, I have chosen to follow its conventions with regard to patriarchal language and male-gendered pronouns, even though personally I disagree with them. I understand that some readers may find this offensive. I cannot argue. I can only ask their tolerance and forgiveness. The one exception to this is my use of the phrase "sisters and brothers" wherever possible in place of the Course's "brothers" (except for quoted passages).

If the Course were to speak to this issue, I suspect it would say something along these lines. Gender is an aspect of the world in which we live. It is a world of appearances, a world of duality, where differences abound and where opposites like female and male are possible. God has no gender. God is not male, female, or neuter. The binary notion of gender begins in the physical body and from there extends to cultural attitudes about which roles and behaviors are "male" and which are "female." Only recently have we begun to challenge these characterizations and realized that gender roles are far more fluid than previously thought. However, God is not a body. God has no body and no concrete physical existence. God is spirit. So are we. Our true nature cannot be defined by limiting constructs like gender. As we already noted, we are love and nothing else.

From Loving One to One Love is a book about the principles of *A Course in Miracles.* The Course was received and scribed by two highly accomplished academic psychologists. Its teachings are so rooted in psychoanalytic theory that prior to Freud it could not have been written. I have studied the Course and tried to put its ideas into practice since the age of twenty. As a semiretired psychiatrist with over three decades of clinical experience, however, I cannot simply ignore all I've learned over the years about couples and relationships. And so in this book about relationships, I have drawn on my experience to introduce psychological concepts that buttress the Course's teachings, which I and many others have found helpful in making relationships more loving. Purists may object that these concepts are not part of the Course proper, and technically they would be correct. Nonetheless, I believe that such concepts are quite compatible with the psychology of *A Course in Miracles.* In fact, had the Course come twenty years later, I have little doubt they would have been included. As with male-gendered pronouns, the Course could not take into account developments in science and society that arrived well after its scribing.

One final note before we begin. *A Course in Miracles* teaches a single truth succinctly expressed in three lines from its introduction:

Nothing real can be threatened.
Nothing unreal exists.
Herein lies the peace of God.

This simple truth is echoed again and again throughout the Course's 1,249 pages in many different forms and variations. Truth is unitary. It has no parts. It is indivisible. However, the world we see is not the world of truth. We are not yet whole. We need multiple approaches to the same core idea if we are to learn effectively. As a result, the Course is repetitive and when writing about the Course a certain degree of repetition is inevitable. Every concept connects to every other in a holographic way. I have done my best to avoid repetition, but it's simply not possible to confine the Course's core teaching to a single chapter or section. It informs everything. It is what we need to hear, again and again, as many times as it takes to break through our defenses and help us awaken to truth.

With that, let's begin!

Part One
Loving One
Relationships

The ark of peace is entered two by two, yet the
beginning of another world goes with them.[1]

1

Introduction

In the summer of 1965, Drs. Bill Thetford and Helen Schucman were struggling. They were colleagues in the department of psychology at Columbia University's College of Physicians and Surgeons in New York. Bill had hired Helen years earlier to help write grant proposals, but the work was not going well, and their interactions with other faculty members in the department were hostile and competitive. Their own relationship offered no solace. Although they deeply respected and cared for each other as colleagues, their interpersonal styles were markedly different. Each seemed to inflame the other's worst characteristics. The most trivial disagreements could rapidly blow up into major battles that left them both with bruised feelings.

To make matters more complicated, Helen was madly in love with Bill. She also happened to be married. Bill did not reciprocate her feelings. He was fourteen years younger and a lifelong bachelor. More to the point, he was a closeted gay male in the homophobic culture of the 1960s. The official *Diagnostic and Statistical Manual* of mental disorders still classified homosexuality as an illness. No wonder Bill chose to keep that aspect of his life hidden. All of this made for a very tumultuous relationship.

One day Bill walked into Helen's office and made an uncharacteristically impassioned plea. Their attitudes had grown so negative, he said, that they couldn't seem to work anything out. "There must be a better way," he told her, and he was determined to find it. Instead of criticizing their colleagues, he would look for the good in them. He would choose collaboration over competition. Bill finished his appeal and waited for Helen's reply. He expected something cynical, but to his amazement, she agreed with him. Better yet, she would join him. Together they committed to finding a better way of relating to people. Their intention at that moment was to apply this new way to their toxic work environment and personal relationship. They had no idea that their joint commitment had set in motion a process with far greater consequences.

In a few short months Helen heard an inner "Voice," as she called it, which she identified as that of Jesus. It "spoke" to her, not in words, but in a rapid stream of thought that she transcribed into words. What it said was, "This is a course in miracles. Please take notes." Helen did just that: she took notes on what she heard and read them to Bill to type up. Seven years later, *A Course in Mira-*

cles was complete. It consisted of three volumes: a Text, a Workbook for Students, and a Manual for Teachers.

Helen and Bill had no idea what it was for. Helen assumed that perhaps five people in the entire world might be mildly interested. Bill suspected it was destined for a wider audience. Over forty years later, the Course they brought into the world has reached over three million people in twenty-seven different languages. There are hundreds of popular books about it, thousands of study groups worldwide, and tens of thousands of dedicated students.

The Path to Awakening

Why share these historical details? Because they demonstrate a significant and often overlooked fact about *A Course in Miracles*: its scribing came in direct response to an appeal for help from two people struggling with their relationship.

As a spiritual system of thought, the Course's focus is not on meditation, prayer, or fasting; other-dimensional experiences; entrancing rituals; or rigorous rules of conduct. It does not prescribe rendering service unto others less fortunate. It is not aimed at changing the world or bettering the lot of the individual self who lives in that world. It is a course in awakening to your true Self. This Self is not the face that stares back at you from the bathroom mirror in the morning. It does not partake of your shifting goals and desires, nor does it understand your fears and the plans you make to avert them—even though it loves you with a love beyond your capacity to understand. Nor does that Self belong to you alone. It belongs equally to everyone.*

In order to awaken to your true Self, you must first unlearn what you believe about your false self. The incubator for this unlearning process is not a mountaintop retreat, a psychedelic drug experience, or a mantra passed down by a guru. It's more prosaic than that, and within reach of just about everyone. The primary vehicle for awakening, according to the Course, is relationship, and one of its central goals is healing conflict in relationship. This can range from the most trivial of disagreements to deadly betrayal. Because in truth, conflict is inherent in all human relationships.

No matter how loving you feel towards someone, if you honestly scrutinize your thoughts about them over the course of a day, you'll find conflict. It comes in the form of judgments, disappointments, disagreements, or a need to control and be right. Although these don't show up all the time, they arise often enough.

It takes two to form a relationship. Two separate individuals come together, each with their own unique backgrounds, worldviews, and goals. Those goals will never precisely match up. They'll often be at odds—as with Helen and her love for Bill. Even when they appear to be in alignment—two lovers absolutely smitten with each other, for example—give it time and they'll diverge. The differences between us inevitably lead to conflict.

---

* The nature of this Self was the topic of the first book in this series, *From Never-Mind to Ever-Mind*.

She wants to go to the movies; he wants to stay home and watch the game. He prefers a comedy; she likes an action film. A father pushes his son to go to medical school and have a good career because he did not; the son just wants to play music with his band. These people love each other. They care deeply for each other. But that does not prevent conflict.

The Course states that "*conflict is the root of all evil*."[1] Yet as we've just seen, conflict is inevitable. So what are we to make of this? Are we all evil? No, of course not. But we are ignorant, and willful in our ignorance. We don't know how to escape conflict because we don't recognize its true cause, and we're unwilling to look deeply into the problem in order to solve it. Into this world of hidden but pervasive conflict comes *A Course in Miracles*. Its curriculum is one of universal love. Sounds good on paper, right? Sign me up! But as we'll see, our resistance to accepting its message of love is massive.

The Course teaches us a way of relating to others in which love is all-encompassing, not special and exclusive: not bestowed upon one and withheld from others. The moment we select someone to love based on *our* preference, we are no longer loving as God loves, unconditionally and universally. These *special relationships*, as the Course calls them, become a barrier to the experience of real love. We can only find real love, and the peace that comes with it, if we are willing to transform our special relationships into *holy relationships*.

Special relationships are transactional in nature, though this is seldom obvious and rarely acknowledged. We want something from someone—something we desire, something special—and we're willing to bargain, sacrifice, or manipulate to get it. It could be something material, like financial support, but far more often it's some quality or characteristic we think they possess and we lack. The other person is kind, affectionate, clever, strong—and we're not. Relationship then becomes a means of fulfilling that lack. By contrast, *holy* relationships have no goal other than letting go of specialness in order to discover the unconditional love that is our essence and lives within us all. When this becomes the purpose of relationship, we awaken to the true Self: the Christ.

According to the Course, God is infinite, expansive, eternal Love—and nothing else. Nothing exists apart from this. Because God created us as an extension of His Being (or "in His image"), we are also infinite, expansive, eternal Love, and nothing else. But somehow we fell into a dream in which an entire world of differences sprang up and God's love seemed to have gone into hiding. At this point, love is no longer a given. It's not natural or universal; it's *special*. Now we have to *do something* in order to be loved. We perform; we play roles. We try to make ourselves appear more attractive, smart, and impressive to convince others that we're worthy of love. But in reality, love is our birthright. It is what we are. It need not be courted or won over. It is with us always. We simply need to remember.

A Course in Miracles teaches us how to do this. It teaches us to shift from special love showered on one special person (whether that's a lover, child, parent, or friend) to universal love, which does not pick favorites but embraces everyone. This love sees itself in everyone. It recognizes the light of holiness that shines in each of us from God. By seeing this in others, we learn to see it in ourselves as well. Now there *is* no more *other*, because we are all one. We are God's creation: His one Son. We have made the shift from many disparate, transactional, one-to-one relationships to a universal joining. We have gone from *loving one* to *One Love*.

*   *   *

This book is about transforming relationships—not at the superficial level, but at their core. We achieve this through forgiveness. However, like so much else in the Course, its concept of forgiveness is very different from the common understanding of the word. You might think of it as *radical forgiveness*—an experience of love and unity so complete, so unblemished, so *not* of this world, that it shines away all sense of differences and any lingering shadows of hurt or recrimination from the past. Such forgiveness goes well beyond the trials we suffer in our individual lives. In its ultimate expression, it dissolves the boundaries that seem to separate us from each other.

In the Bible, we are told that Jesus instructed us to love your neighbor as yourself. This seems like an impossible and preposterous task. How can you love criminals? Murderers? How can you love that politician when it makes you sick just to listen to him? How can you love those who do not love you back? And how can you love those who've hurt you or someone you love? The world has no answer. But the Course does. Forgiveness is the answer. It is the key to understanding how these things are possible and then putting them into practice.

Clearly, the Course sets a high bar. Many, perhaps most, have zero interest in learning to love the way Jesus taught. But they do want to improve the relationships they already have. That may not qualify them for sainthood, but it's a worthwhile goal and a big step in the right direction. The simple fact is, forgiveness is the cure for what ails every relationship. Whether your problems seem great or small, a momentary glitch or a life-threatening assault, forgiveness reveals them to you in a different light. It helps you to remember love, to see through the veil of hurt and recrimination to the truth, and to reclaim your true Self.

To whatever extent you're able to apply forgiveness, your relationships will improve. Conflict gives way to peace. Difficult people will become easier. You might even find you like them. Often there will be no rational explanation for the change. And here's the most inexplicable thing: you don't have to do anything. Forgiveness is not about taking action. It's about changing your mind.

The Course is clear that the mind is the only reality. What you see "out there" in the world is simply a very convincing projection of what's in your mind. Therefore, when you take responsibility for how you see someone and change your mind about them—when you look at them through the healing lens of forgiveness—at some deep level they cannot help but feel it and respond. They must change too.

Forgiveness improves relationships, but that's not its only benefit. The consistent practice of forgiveness reshapes your own sense of what you are. You can no longer see yourself as the victim of random external circumstances. Nor can you view yourself as an independent agent disconnected from others: "you go your way and I'll go mine." You discover that at the level of the mind, we are all interconnected. *"Forgiveness lets me know that minds are joined."*[2] Knowing this, it becomes your responsibility to "mind the mind" and make it a welcoming, loving place—for you and for all those you love and will come to love.

Review of Book One and *A Course in Miracles*

Before proceeding, I'd like to remind readers that this is the *second* book in a series on the principles of *A Course in Miracles*. You will find it easier to understand if you've already read the first book, *From Never-Mind to Ever-Mind: Transforming the Self to Embrace Miracles*—and more importantly, if you've already started studying the Course itself. However, for those in need of a recap, what follows is a brief summary of the key points from this first book and from the Course's own teachings.

Know Thyself

I toss a yellow squeaky toy shaped like a bone to the opposite side of the living room. My dog chases after it in delight while my cat looks on, befuddled by such antics. She prefers to meticulously stalk the small bird that's had the bad luck to settle on our lawn—something the dog would never have the patience for. Their happiness is particular to their natures. Neither would be satisfied with the other's lot. Happiness comes from knowing and accepting what you are.

A Course in Miracles tells us that the key question everyone must answer is: *what am I?* Without that knowledge, there is no hope of finding real happiness. In *From Never-Mind to Ever-Mind*, we looked deeply into this question of self. We systematically reviewed the conventional ways in which we identify the self and discovered that they simply don't hold up. They turn out to be window dressing for something far more difficult to grasp.

The fact is, you do *not* know yourself—not your true self. Very few of us have that awareness. The self you believe to be *you* is an elaborate fiction woven together from many different strands, such as your name, physical appearance, the values and beliefs you hold, and the different roles you play in the course of a lifetime. Nor is your true self in any way related to that persistent nagging voice inside your head that force-feeds you a running commentary on everything you think and do. The true Self has no relation to the stories from your past, which you've collected in memory and which, patched together, seem to make up your personal history—the timeline of your life on earth. None of these speak to the essence of your being. None are *you*. They are simply aspects of a construct that in my first book I dubbed *Never-Mind,* because they can *never* represent the true extent of what you are and in God's reality they *never* existed at all. The Course does not use the term *Never-Mind*. Preferring the language of psychoanalysis, it refers to this impostor self as *the ego*. In this book, so will I.

Because you are fully identified with the ego and treasure the empty gifts it seems to offer, you remain oblivious to your true identity. But that doesn't mean it's not there. You haven't lost that Self. That's not possible, because God created it and you have no power to overrule God and undo His creation. But you can overlook that Self. You can choose to gaze into a mirage that's so compelling that you value it over reality.

In practical terms, why is it so important to "know thyself"? Because unless you know your true nature—who and what you are—and live your life from that knowingness, unless that becomes the wellspring of your very being, you will encounter hardship and suffering. You'll be paddling upstream. You will not find satisfaction, certainly not in any lasting sense. And at the end, you—the *you* that you believed yourself to be, the ego-self that you trusted to guide you and keep you safe—will die. It is not possible to achieve real, enduring happiness if you accept this flawed and fleeting identity as your self. You cannot arrive at truth by starting out from a false premise.

According to *A Course in Miracles*, your true Self has nothing to do with the person you think you are, the life you imagine you're living, or the things you strive for and hold dear. Your true Self abides outside of time and space, independent of matter. It is pure spirit: eternal, changeless, peaceful, joyous, and wholly loving. In the previous book, I called it *Ever-Mind* in contrast to Never-Mind. The Course calls it the *Christ* or the *Sonship*. This Self, the Christ, lives within you, but not in you alone. You share this holy Identity with every other living thing. In fact, it cannot be known until you recognize that it is shared.

This shared identity is reflected here in the world by our desire to join together in groups. We temporarily set aside our individual agendas in service of a common purpose. We want to be part of something greater, whether that's a sports team, a high-school play, a church community, a protest march, or a world-changing movement. We may be captivated by the dizzying array of possibilities the world puts before us, but we are always drawn towards union.

Nonetheless, worldly groups almost always end up mirroring the sense of separation and the resulting competition that is characteristic of all things in this world. The only thing capable of bringing everyone together under one common purpose is what the Course calls the *Atonement*: God's universal answer for the imagined "sin" of separation and its consequences. *"Atonement is the one need in this world that is universal."*[3] Among prisoners, the only cause that truly unites everyone is escape.

The goal of *A Course in Miracles* then is not some dry intellectual understanding. The Course trains us in a very practical manner to remember our true nature as the Christ or Ever-Mind; to reinstate this greater Self as our primary identity, even in this world; to experience that Self without fear or resistance; to acknowledge its presence in everyone; and ultimately to return to it in oneness and love. The result of this learning is a degree of happiness and peace that is beyond imagining and would otherwise remain forever out of reach.

What Is the World?

Another consequence inevitably results from accepting the ego as self: by identifying with it and letting it rule your life, you have chosen to live within its world. However, because the ego is not real, neither is the world that arises from it. According to the Course, this world that you experience all around you every day—the world brought to you by your five senses—is an illusion, a mass hallucination. It does not and cannot exist independently of the mind. You might think of it as a virtual-reality simulation projected from your mind in much the same way as a movie is projected onto a blank screen: "*the outside picture of an inward condition.*"[4] The Course states that "*perception is a mirror, not a fact.*"[5] The world reflects back to us exactly what we want to see in it. And what we see is no blissful picnic.

A Course in Miracles is very clear: Reality is determined by God. Only what He creates is real. God did not create the world of perception. God did not create the billions of humans and trillions of different life forms that inhabit earth. How could absolute Oneness and Love make a world of separate parts defined by differences, a world containing so much suffering? How could what is eternal create a limit on itself in the form of death?

We made this world. It is a wild, mad thought that the Son of God dwelt upon for a mere instant, one that exploded into an entire world of time and space. In this sense, the Big Bang, which produced the physical universe, was equivalent to the biblical Fall that expelled Adam and Eve from

Eden into the hard, cruel world. But whether you think of it as the Big Bang, the Fall, or the Course's preferred term, the *separation* (from God), it gave rise to the dream world of contrasts and opposites in which we live. Hot and cold, good and bad, pain and pleasure, life and death—all seem real now. This is our virtual-reality prison. The Course provides us with a key so we can let ourselves out.

The world we inhabit is not the will of God. But we cannot eradicate God or replace Him entirely, however much the ego might wish it. That is beyond our ability. Remember, God created us; we did not create God. And so there is also joy and love in the world, but it is obscure, and it does not last. It is always vulnerable to change and loss. Our fleeting experiences of love are but the faintest, most remote glimmer of the blazing, all-encompassing Love that is God.

The idea that the world is an illusion of our own making is hard to accept, even for some Course students. Instead we prefer to cling to the notion that we are individual beings struggling to do our best in a world that's all too real. In this world, we have no doubt that we are separate from each other and from God (if God even exists). Certain people are on our side and help us; others are rivals, enemies who stand in the way of what we want. But friends can turn into enemies overnight, and the goals we worked so hard to achieve can vanish in an instant when death comes knocking. This is insanity, and it afflicts us all. We are delusional, wandering an illusory world in a fugue state, unable to remember our true identity or our Creator.

God could not have created such a world. God cannot even understand it. How could the Source of all reality comprehend what is unreal and incomprehensible? Nor is God responsible for what goes on in this world. He does not oversee or control events. Sparrows may drop by the thousands; it has nothing to do with God. God does not choose the winner of the World Cup or Super Bowl, no matter how impassioned the pregame prayers. *Nothing* that happens here has *anything* to do with God—except for love.

But God did not abandon us to our delusional nightmare. God created an answer to the separation, a pathway back to Reality, a bridge that will enable us to cross the chasm between illusion and truth. God created a guide to lead us home, a friend who will gently help us to awaken from the feverish dream that has held our collective minds captive. The Course calls this guide the *Holy Spirit.* "*The Holy Spirit is God's Answer to the separation; the means by which the Atonement heals.*"[6]

When we choose to follow the Holy Spirit's guidance, He brings our minds back into accord with our true Self. When this Self is firmly established in us and the separate ego is recognized for the nothingness it is, the world of time and space comes to its end in a blaze of love, and we return wholly and happily to God.

2

The Necessity of Relationships

Samuel Johnson said something to the effect that nothing concentrates the mind like the prospect of a hanging. Faced with imminent, unavoidable death, our priorities change drastically. We see what's of vital importance and what we no longer give a hoot about. If satisfied with the life we've lived—if we feel complete—we can discover an unexpected sense of peace and freedom in the anticipation of death. If not, there will be regret, often crippling and bitter.

Early in my psychiatric career, I consulted to the oncology ward of a large inner-city hospital. As you might expect, this mostly involved diagnosing and treating depression. But it also gave me the opportunity to engage with people in the final stage of life and help them make peace with the fact that they were dying.

Among the many patients I met with during that time, there was not a single one who regretted that they hadn't made more money or that they'd once blown a major business deal or a lucrative investment opportunity. Yet again and again I heard tales of sadness about a son or daughter who had become estranged over some insignificant argument decades earlier; a good friend with whom they'd failed to stay in touch; or a parent or child with whom they wished they'd spent more quality time when they had the chance and to whom they should have said, "I love you," "I'm so proud of you," "I appreciate you," far more often than they did. These are the pangs that haunt us when we stand at the precipice of death and peer back over the landscape of our lives. Relationships, love, appreciation—these are the things that matter in the end.

Take a minute to pause and survey your thoughts about the day ahead: your concerns and expectations, the things that both upset and delight you. Which of these do *not* involve relationships in some way? With few exceptions, relationships are the most important thing in life. Healthy or unhealthy, supportive or draining, our relationships give life its meaning.

The Price of Isolation

Psychologists have long been aware of the detrimental impact of isolation on infants. In orphanages around the world, babies who are held often and loved by their caregivers will thrive, while those left alone, deprived of human touch, will wither and die. Our very survival depends on this most basic sense of connection.

A friend of mine tells a powerful story about a baby girl who attended the same day-care center as her daughter. Every afternoon she'd arrive to pick up her daughter, and she'd see this quiet little baby sitting off by herself, swinging back and forth in a mechanical rocker, isolated from the other children and untouched by the caregivers. When she demanded to know why they were neglecting this child, they told her that the child's parents insisted on this arrangement. They didn't want their daughter to grow up "spoiled" from too much attention.

One day my friend arrived to find the day-care center in an uproar and the caregivers in tears. Earlier that day, and for no apparent medical reason, this baby girl had died. All her material needs had been met; she had plenty of food and drink and warm clothing. But she was starved of touch, of connection, and of that most basic human need—relationship.

Isolation is always painful, although once we make it past infancy, it is rarely fatal in the way it was for that baby girl. Nonetheless, people who report feeling lonely are more likely to be depressed, have more medical problems, and are at greater risk of suicide. On the other hand, married couples and those with close ties to family and friends live longer, healthier lives. In recognition of loneliness as a growing societal problem, the United Kingdom recently established a Minister for Loneliness. Although many scoffed at the notion, it represents an attempt to address the loneliness that is rampant and growing, particularly among seniors.

If you experienced loving touch and a consistent sense of warm connection early in life, that pattern of healthy attachment becomes integrated as part of your being. You've learned that you are welcome in the world, you are wanted, you belong. This feeling becomes part of your sense of self and remains with you forever after. As an adult, you don't need to be held every day or greeted with a smile every morning (although that's always nice) to know you're loved and worthwhile. It's as if you have your own internal reservoir of relatedness that will see you safely through times of isolation and loneliness.

On the other hand, if you were deprived of love and connection in your early years, you have no inner template for relatedness. You may distrust others, and that distrust breeds distrust in those around you so that they avoid you. This in turn validates your distrust: "I knew it. They don't like me." You see yourself as isolated, someone who has to make it on your own in a harsh world, someone who must fight others for what's yours. Your relationships are not warm or caring. They're all about what you can get from others. Instead of valuing love and connection, your life goals are likely to focus on material things. These at least are certain. An object will never snub you.

If we look at these two very different approaches to life and relationships, it's clear which offers the greater satisfaction. We need relationships. We want relationships that work, where love is welcomed and shared, and conflict is minimized. There is no substitute for this.

A Nexus of Relationships

We are born into a world dense with relationships: parents and grandparents, siblings, aunts and uncles—all there to greet us whether we like it or not. As we grow and our lives expand beyond the borders of family into school and work, we acquire new relationships: friends, lovers, mentors, colleagues, rivals. But rarely do we think of ourselves in those terms. We swim in a sea of relatedness, yet still we consider ourselves separate individuals interacting with other individuals.

In *From Never-Mind to Ever-Mind,* I explored the tension between the individual self and the group. Which one is the true self? In nature, is the solo ant the actual organism, or is it the bustling ant colony? The lone wolf or the wolf pack? Even within the physical body, what is the relationship among individual cells, the organs, and the whole? Which is the real *you*? Which is *self*?

Nature is composed of hierarchical systems of organization nested within each other. Atoms combine to form molecules. Molecules become cells. Cells aggregate into tissues and organs, which together constitute the body. Those bodies interrelate in families, communities, nations. At each level we can turn our focus on either the individual or the collective, the part or the whole, but neither is truly accurate. Neither captures the whole picture, because what appears to be whole can be broken down into its component parts, while at the same time the separate parts can join and give rise to something greater.

Everything in this world exists in relationship to something else. It's not possible to single out any individual part, at any level of organization, and regard it as complete unto itself—not without losing sight of the bigger picture.

Relationships are not all uniform, however. They can be helpful or harmful, healing or destructive. If helpful, the parts work together for their mutual benefit. In biology, this is called *symbiosis*.

Symbiotic relationships are essential to life. For example, the native bacteria that live in your gut obtain nutrients from the food you eat; in return they create a stable chemical environment that makes it harder for pathogenic bacteria to invade the body. Both you and the native bacteria profit. At a higher level of organization, a start-up pharmaceutical company develops a promising new drug and enters into a deal with a larger, more established corporation to market and distribute their drug in return for a share of the profits. Each is willing to give something to the other to achieve a goal that is of benefit to both and that neither could accomplish on its own.

Unfortunately, not all relationships in nature are symbiotic. Many are destructive. A virus invades a cell and hijacks its DNA to produce more viruses. Swim in certain African rivers, and you risk contracting the disease schistosomiasis: tiny fluke larvae enter your body through the pores of your skin and lay eggs that colonize your body's organs. These are parasitic relationships. The parasite takes what *it* needs for itself, but gives nothing of value back to its host in return. On the contrary, its actions harm the host. As a result, parasitic relationships are unsustainable. They self-destruct, because eventually the parasite consumes all the host's resources or damages the host so extensively that it dies. When the host dies, the parasites die too. They've lost their source of sustenance. The relationship proves fatal to them both.

Human relationships tend to fall into these same categories. If one person uses the other and gives nothing back, if
they manipulate and take what they desire until nothing is
left, then the relationship dies. Others are symbiotic, with
each partner happily contributing to the benefit of both.
But unless giving is motivated by love, the relationship will
devolve over time and become purely transactional. The
symbiotic balance may endure for a while, for example in a
business deal that's good for both parties, but without love,
it is vulnerable to change and ultimately unsustainable.

The parasitic relationship kills, because it can only
take. By contrast, the symbiotic relationship supports life
through mutual giving and receiving, especially when that
giving comes from love.

Giving and Receiving

A Course in Miracles has a lot to say about symbiosis,
though it never uses that word. Instead it talks about giving and receiving. It tells us that in God's Reality giving
and receiving are one and the same process. *"To give and to
receive are one in truth."*[1] This makes no sense in our separated state, where, when we give something to another, we
no longer have it for ourselves. But it makes perfect sense in
the oneness of the true Self, the Ever-Mind, where there is
no separation or division and where only love exists. Oneness can only give, and only to itself because there *is* nothing else. Nothing else exists. Oneness has no separate parts
to take the roles of giver and receiver. For this reason, the

Course can state in Workbook lesson 126: *"All that I give is given to my Self."*

Giving and receiving occur simultaneously, because in eternity there is no past or future, only the present. They are dual aspects of a process that appears to be sequential, because we regard giving and receiving as opposite actions taking place at different times.

An old tale about heaven and hell illustrates this principle beautifully. You have been invited to tour heaven and hell. You are led to two rooms identical in every respect except that one is hell, the other heaven. You open the door to hell, and inside you see a large table piled high with sumptuous food of all variety. Seated around the table are those condemned to suffer for all eternity. Each has been given a long spoon, which they must use to feed themselves. They can reach the food easily enough and scoop it up, but their utensils are too long to get any of that tasty food back into their mouths. They twist and turn, trying in vain to eat. They will spend eternity starved and tortured, staring at a banquet that is forever beyond reach.

In the adjacent room you find the residents of heaven. They are gathered around exactly the same table with the same delicious dishes and the same overly long spoons. But in this room, they do not attempt to feed themselves. With great delight, they use their spoons to reach across the table and feed those opposite them, while those fortunate souls return the favor and offer food from their spoons. Everyone gets to eat to their heart's delight. No one goes without. Heaven is shared; hell is solitary.

Of course, the giving of things, of objects or services, is very different from the giving of ideas. Things are material; they can only be given by bodies. When the thing leaves your hand, you lose it. By contrast, *ideas do not leave their source*, as the Course states several times. If I share an idea with you—a good joke, for example—I don't lose it. I enjoy your laughter, and then we both have the joke to share with others. The joke extends its reach, and neither of us has to be deprived of it.

The same holds true for love. If I give you love, I don't lose it. No one can be diminished by loving.

As we said, *A Course in Miracles* teaches that only mind exists. God is Mind. We are mind. And God is Love. Therefore love is not something we *do* with or to another. It exists at the level of mind. It is an idea we share. When we give love, it unites us, because it reminds us of our true Identity, the one Self we share, created by the Love that is God. The Course tells us that love *must* extend. That is its nature. That is how God created us: by extending the Love that is His Being. Love is what we *are*.

Here on earth we love imperfectly, but we cannot *not* love. The ego can try to suppress love, and it certainly tries to convince us that it has better things to offer (including, as we'll see, its own special brand of "love"). But it cannot eradicate love, because that is our true nature. The illusion of love cannot triumph over its reality.

In the mystical perfect moment (described in chapter 3 of *From Never-Mind to Ever-Mind*), love simply *is*. It's an abstraction in need of no object. It overspreads and permeates everything. This is how the Self that is our true Identity loves. Few of us are capable of that as yet. For us, love blossoms in relationships. That is the focus of this book: how to form truly loving relationships; how to make our current relationships more loving; and then, once we've managed that, learning how to love as God loves.

Love in an Imperfect World

Although God and Love are the essence of what we are, we are far from being able to love as God loves. Instead we seek love from others through our relationships, and we fall short. Even in relationships where love should come easily—with those we already claim to love—we cannot remain consistently loving. All too often we are triggered into anger or disappointment. We can be mean-spirited or outright nasty. And all too often the love we share feels unequal, unsatisfying, out of balance somehow—as if some key ingredient were missing. We still *love* our partner, of course, but we no longer feel much connection. Not like we used to. We don't feel *seen* by them. We don't feel that they know us anymore.

Love as we commonly understand it is rarely enough to sustain a long-term committed relationship. You cannot simply say "I love you" every morning and walk off certain that your relationship is secure. We seek other things from our partners as well. You might think of them as derivatives of love: love's companions here in the ego's imperfect world, where separation seems to rule. If our relationships are to become ever more loving, then we need to cultivate these things as well: mutual appreciation, transparency, and above all, intimacy.

*   *   *

Everyone wants to be appreciated. We want to be appreciated for who we really are, not for the face we show the world. Easy praise that's ladled out indiscriminately does not satisfy this need, nor does slavish idolization. Put me on a pedestal, and I won't feel appreciated; I'll worry about falling off.

In addition to appreciation, we want to be *seen*, that is, to be accepted as we are and not judged. We want our partners to look deeply, caringly, and honestly into our eyes, our hearts, our souls, and to say yes to what they see there. And we want them to let us see into them in the same deep way. We want this two-way transparency. From transparency comes trust, and without trust there can be no love.

Transparency is a rare quality in relationships, because it requires a willingness to be vulnerable, to reveal what lives within you without resistance or reservation. What you keep hidden from your partner becomes a divide. Secrets block transparency; you can't see past them. When you refuse to share, you tear a hole in the fabric of the relationship. These holes don't repair themselves; they get bigger over time. Eventually they grow so large that they swallow the relationship entirely. Nothing real remains.

By contrast, if we cultivate transparency with our partner, the result is intimacy. We are seen and known, even if the process exposes certain things about us that make us uncomfortable. Another human being has borne witness to our flaws and in spite of them accepted and appreciated us for who we are. Far better to be *seen*, to be *known,* flaws and all, than to hide who we are and settle for a charade of smiles and superficial approval. After all, how can we be loved and appreciated for ourselves if we're not willing to reveal that self fully?

You might think of the word *intimacy* as *into-me-see.* Let me open up to you and share with you my deepest fears and secrets as well as my private joys. And allow me the honor to peer deeply into you, trusting that I will hold what I see in you with the same respect and willingness to love as you have shown me. I see into you and you see into me. In that joining, that honesty, that trust, love must flourish.

Our need for appreciation, transparency, and intimacy, if understood properly, reflects a deeper need to be recognized for what we truly are: not mere humans but God's perfect Son. Although few of us realize it, this is our secret longing, and it shows up in every significant relationship we have. We are hungry to be *seen* and *known*—by ourselves, our partners, and by God. We need to know that God still recognizes us and has not forgotten us, that God's love is with us always despite our many flaws. It is this unconditional love we seek for and hope to find in our intimate relationships.

*   *   *

Not all relationships are created equal. At this writing, there are over seven billion people and counting on planet earth. You will personally meet only a tiny fraction of them. And most of those encounters will be superficial: schoolmates, coworkers, service providers, people affiliated with some group you belong to, and so on. You may learn their names and a bit about what they do, but not much more. Only a handful of your relationships will be truly intimate. This is unavoidable. Who could function if they sought for intimacy in *all* of their relationships? It would be exhausting and would require far more time than any of us have in one life.

In his seminal work *I and Thou*, theologian Martin Buber proposed that all human relationships fall into two categories which he labeled *I-It* and *I-Thou*. The *I-It* relationship is akin to that between two or more objects. Objects can be related by proximity, shape, size, class, purpose, and so on. So too can human beings. We join on the basis of what we have in common. But *I-Thou* is different.

Buber wrote in German, which, like many languages, employs two forms of the English pronoun *you*: one formal, the other familiar. In German, these are *Sie* and *du*. The English translation of the German *du* is *thou*. But unless you're a nineteenth-century Quaker, the word *thou* feels awkward: stilted and churchy rather than warm and intimate. We are likely to associate it with the King James Version of the Bible, where it has come to convey a sense of reverence and therefore, ironically, distance rather than closeness. The intimacy of the German *du* is literally lost in translation.

We seek the intimacy of I-Thou in our closest relationships. As we saw, this requires a commitment to transparency. And yet how often do we allow such transparency?

How often are we willing to commit to the goal of *into-me-see*? If we're honest, we will admit that, as much as we want it, we're also afraid of it. We prefer to retreat into a fantasy of love in which we set someone up as special—an idol, really—and worship them, calling this "love." If they return this worship, then we have achieved a facsimile of love without ever having to risk exposing what lies within. We have embraced the ego's darling and entered into what *A Course In Miracles* calls the *special relationship*.

3

The Special Love Relationship

A young man crashes the big masquerade party hosted by his aristocratic family's enemies, only to fall madly in love with their beautiful daughter. A young woman and her possessive high-society fiancé embark on a transatlantic cruise—the maiden voyage of the world's biggest ocean liner—where she meets and falls in love with an endearing young artist well below her station. The obstacles that stand in the way of their love are daunting, but the young lovers do their utmost to overcome them. The pull of true love is irresistible.

Four centuries separate Shakespeare's *Romeo and Juliet* and James Cameron's film *Titanic*, yet both have found an enduring place in the human psyche for their portrayal of romantic love. Juliet leaning over her balcony, flirting with Romeo, who courts her from below; Rose, leaning out over the frothing ocean from the bow of the *Titanic*, gripped firmly and lovingly in the arms of Jack, experiencing something her wealthy fiancé could never have given her—these scenes live on in our minds. Why? What makes romantic love so compelling, so irresistible, a goal to be pursued above all others?

The primacy of romantic love is underscored by the double story line in the film *Titanic*. The modern-day treasure hunters search for the sunken ship and the priceless diamond necklace that was lost somewhere within its wreckage. This is their goal, the thing that gives their lives meaning. On the other hand, the now-elderly Rose (who possessed the missing necklace all along) finds in her recollections the real treasure: the love she shared with Jack, a love that she'd forced herself to forget, but could now reclaim by sharing her story with the treasure hunters.

In tales like these, we identify with the lovers. We share their longing, their hopes, their plans, their joy. We want what they want. Because, we think, if you can't experience that sort of undying passion even once in a lifetime, then what's the point of it all?

Romeo and Juliet, Rose and Jack, epitomize what *A Course in Miracles* calls *the special love relationship*. The Course says, "*The special love relationship is the ego's chief weapon for keeping you from Heaven.*"[1] But wait! Isn't this relationship supposed to *be* heaven—or at least as close to it as we can get in this world? If you find true love as these lovers did, then isn't your life is complete?

At best, romantic love is intense but fleeting, even desperate. Romeo and Juliet, Jack and Rose only knew each other a short while. Their fiery romance feels undying to us because we know the story. The story lives on, yet ironically, it is enshrined and made permanent only through the lovers' deaths.

Imagine a different ending in which the lovers do not die. Instead Romeo and Juliet make their marriage public and bring peace to their feuding families. They have children, some of whom in that era would die, while others would survive only to rebel. The lovers grow old, overweight, and forgetful. As for Jack and Rose, instead of a frozen goodbye, they get married, have a bunch of kids, and fight over not having enough money to support them in the manner she'd like. Perhaps she even looks back wistfully and fantasizes about the life she could have lived in the lap of luxury. Would their stories still hold their appeal? You know the answer. Like those star-crossed teenage lovers, romantic love is doomed from the start. An iceberg called death lies submerged in the dark waters ahead, and it is inescapable.

Romantic love is a myth, a mayfly that lives for the space of a day, perhaps, then must pass. That's its appeal. It's as if romantic love really could stop time and freeze us in an ideal instant that never ends, in which we love and are loved back fully and equally. But eternity is not the gift of the special relationship. As we'll see, that comes only from God and the Holy Spirit. The ego's "gift" is death—death because the ego cannot last; because "happily ever after" is a bromide to help children fall sleep; because, like all things in this world of time, such love must change and pass and come to an end.

Lovers need not commit suicide for their love to perish. The moment the special love relationship veers off into the routine, its demise is certain. When you awaken each morning to your partner's bad breath; when you're forced to put up with their sloppiness or their compulsive need for order, their temper outbursts or depressive slumps; when you struggle against their reckless spending or their tight-fisted refusal to pony up for even the most ordinary expenses, then whatever specialness you once glimpsed in them begins to dim, eclipsed by the reality of their day-to-day self.

Mike Nichols' classic 1967 film *The Graduate* gives special love the kind of ending it's more likely to encounter in the world outside the movies. Ben (played by Dustin Hoffman) has been pursuing Elaine (played by Katharine Ross) on and off throughout the movie. In the climactic scene, he shows up at her wedding, crying out her name from the church balcony and pounding on a heavy glass barrier that separates him from the wedding party and muffles his shouts. A more visual portrayal of the obstacles standing in the way of "true love" is hard to imagine. Elaine responds and together they flee the church, she in her wedding gown, he a disheveled wreck. They climb aboard a city transit bus. In the final shot of the film, they're seated side by side at the back of the bus. The long pursuit is over. They've done it; they've finally gotten together. Love has triumphed over all obstacles.

Slowly, their elation fades and ambiguity creeps in. Ben stares ahead vacantly. Elaine darts a curious look at him and when he fails to notice, turns and stares blankly ahead herself, mirroring him. Instead of the happily-ever-after stroll into the sunset, both face the big question mark that represents their future together. It's unsettling. Not what they or the audience anticipated. Not exactly what they wanted after all.

Special love dies, but the desire for it does not. *You just chose poorly,* you rationalize to yourself. *Next time you'll do better.* But like Tantalus, the Titan from Greek mythology whose punishment was to hunger after fruit on a bough that was forever just beyond reach, the moment you sense that the love you seek may be within your grasp, it will elude you. It will change to something else, something more mundane. It must, because unlike God's love, special love does not last.

Of course, not all relationships fit this model. Two people can begin a relationship as friends and grow together into a love based on mutual caring and respect. This is exactly what takes place in many arranged marriages, and may explain why they tend to be more stable and enduring, despite the fact that neither partner ever fell in love with the other. Two people can also come together with the shared purpose of supporting each other in their emotional or spiritual growth. Whatever then occurs between them—however difficult or challenging—becomes grist for the mill of mutual awakening.

Like the ego and everything it offers, the special love relationship turns out to be a sham. Sham love does not satisfy. Like sugar or caffeine, it provides a temporary jolt of energy and excitement. But who can survive on a diet of jelly beans and espresso? Also like sugar and caffeine, special love is addictive. It leads to further craving. For many, the search for true love becomes an endless quest, because in the ego's world, there will always be someone "better," someone more special, who can finally "complete" you. *Your soul mate is out there waiting,* the ego whispers. *Don't give up. Keep searching and one day you will find them.* Yet when you do find "the one" you've been searching for, it's guaranteed that at some point, in some way, they will disappoint you. They will fail to live up to some expectation of yours. You'll begin to question whether they're really so special after all.

This is the problem with tying love to specialness. Specialness is relative; we know it only by comparison. And comparison is an ego device for maintaining the belief that others are separate and different from you. By contrast, the love of our true Self is all-encompassing. It sees no differences and therefore can make no comparisons. In its light no one is judged and seen as special; everyone is recognized and welcomed as holy. Yet we rarely choose this love. We prefer the chase for specialness.

Here we have a prime example of the ego's dictum: "*Seek and do* not *find.*"[2] The ego does not want you to give up on special love. It needs you to keep searching. However, like the drunk who searches for his keys under a streetlight, where he did not lose them, you cannot find love outside yourself. Why not? Because *you are the love you seek* and you cannot *be* outside yourself.

As long as love depends on attracting someone else, you maintain the illusion that you are separate from them and separate from love. You continue to believe that love can be found only within the ego's dream, and so you remain captive to that dream—which is the ego's goal. "*The special love relationship is an attempt to bring love into separation.*

And, as such, it is nothing more than an attempt to bring love into fear, and make it real in fear." [3]

The separation was a descent from love into fear. The special love relationship cannot escape the taint of that fear, however much it pretends to. When you find yourself strongly attracted to someone, what do you experience? Your knees go weak, your mouth goes dry, you get a funny feeling in the pit in your stomach, your pupils dilate. Adrenaline is rushing through your system. These are the body's responses to fear! The attraction of special love is the attraction to fear. We're climbing on board a roller coaster, but there's no guarantee that the ride will be safe. Attraction and the fear of its loss are simultaneous. "What if he/she doesn't like me?" Scarier still, "what if they *do*? What then?"

In the separation we believed our connection to love was lost. The special relationship merely replays that loss. Being of the ego, it cannot do otherwise. As a tool of the ego, it tries to redefine love in terms of fear and in that way make it appealing and real.

Obviously love is not fear. Love is not separation. Love *is* real; fear and separation are illusions. Without the ego's obfuscations, no one could possibly confuse the two. Love comes from awakening, not from chasing after yet another dream within the dream.

The Anatomy of Specialness

Romeo and Juliet, Rose and Jack—these are not real people. They are characters in a story. They offer us an appealing fantasy of romantic love, one that keeps us thirsting and searching. Their story, however, is not ours. The reality of the special love relationship is something altogether different from such fantasies.

The key to understanding the special relationship lies in your choice of a partner. The object of the ego's "love" is always someone whom it regards as special—which is to say, more special than you. They seem to possess some quality, some ability or status, that you believe you lack. It could be anything: beauty, brains, success, a terrific family, fun friends. It could also be pain, pathos, and suffering that draw you to them. Or it could simply be that *they* see in *you* something they think *they* lack. Something wonderful. Something special. Something you never thought you had. In all instances, the ego believes that this special person possesses some attribute that it lacks and wants for itself. The relationship becomes a form of barter in the wares of specialness—*you give me what I need, and I'll give you what you need.* The ego evaluates all of its relationships as desirable or not solely on this basis: what does the other person have that I do not? And if they give me what I lack, what will they demand in return?

I recall falling in love once as a teen because an attractive girl at a party locked eyes with me and smiled. *She likes me,* I thought. *She thinks I'm special.* Which of course made her special too. A few years later I fell in love with a woman because she seemed to have so much more life experience than I did—even though that experience consisted of suffering through years of an abusive marriage. It didn't matter. It made her special—in ways both positive and negative. Her hard-won experience would compensate for my inexperience. In return, I would save her—wounded bird that she was—through my gentle caring and decency. I would love her as her ex could not.

Of course, this special something that we see in another is almost always a fantasy. Because the ego is incomplete, it never sees anyone else as complete either. It focuses only on those aspects of the other that it *wants* to see. It selects out certain positive attributes while ignoring others that do not fit the image and might undermine the lure of special-ness. *She's amazingly sweet. Everybody loves her. I'd like to be loved that way.* Or *he's so confident, so sure in his opinions. He doesn't care what anyone else thinks. I wish I could be more like that.* The ego believes that the best way to gain these missing ingredients for itself is to fall in love, win over this remarkable individual, and hold on to them for-ever. Remember the song "Some Enchanted Evening" from Rodgers' and Hammerstein's musical *South Pacific*: "Once you have found her, never let her go."

The ego's reasoning goes something like this: *If I can convince this special person to love me, then I'll be special too. I'll bask vicariously in the glow of their specialness. As long as they stay with me, no one will see what I lack. Instead they'll see how remarkable I am because this special person has cho-sen* me *as their partner.* In the romantic comedy film *Jerry Maguire*, Tom Cruise's character tells Renée Zellweger's, "I love you. You complete me." That could be the ego's motto for special love. *You complete me.*

To the extent that we regard ourselves as lacking, this notion of completion is very appealing. As fractured beings split off from the oneness of our Creator, of course we want completion in the form of union. But is specialness really the glue that repairs our damaged self? Or does it serve instead to harden the fissures in our oneness? Can anything from the ego's world knit together what the ego itself has broken?

This need for completion is rarely conscious. We don't enter a relationship thinking about what we lack and what the other might supply. That would be too obviously mercantile. Rather, it plays out unconsciously in the form of attraction. Think of it as the real "law of attraction." We're drawn most powerfully to those who seem to have what we believe we lack.

And so it is that two people fall in love and embark on a special relationship. It is exclusive to the two of them, their own private bubble world, in which they attempt to reinvent paradise. It's an island fortress walled off from everyone but themselves. No one else may enter, because that could threaten their dream of specialness. Someone else might catch the scent and steal specialness from them. Or one of the lovers might discover that someone else is even more special; they might choose to leave.

A Course in Miracles describes the special love relationship as "*a strange and unnatural ego device*"[4] that's really not about the other person at all, but is rather a futile attempt to achieve completion for the incomplete ego self through sacrifice.

> *Most curious of all is the concept of the self which the ego fosters in the special relationship. This "self" seeks the relationship to make itself complete. Yet when it finds the special*

relationship in which it thinks it can accomplish this it gives itself away, and tries to "trade" itself for the self of another. This is not union, for there is no increase or extension. Each partner tries to sacrifice the self he does not want for one he thinks he would prefer. And he feels guilty for the "sin" of taking, and of giving nothing of value in return. How much value can he place upon a self that he would give away to get a "better" one?

The "better" self the ego seeks is always one that is more special. And whoever seems to possess a special self is "loved" for what can be taken from him. Where both partners see this special self in each other, the ego sees "a union made in Heaven." [5]

This model of relationship is the ego's darling. The Course tells us it is the ego's answer to the Holy Spirit's plan of Atonement. *Forget about God and all that oneness nonsense. Here is the love you really want. God can't love you as special, not ever, but this remarkable individual can and will.*

The ego longs for such specialness. Its shadowy presence is felt to some degree in every attempt at relationship, from the crassest drunken sexual hookup to the lofty ideal of pure, chaste love at a distance that medieval knights proffered to their chosen maidens. In the mind of the ego, this becomes life's ultimate achievement: to find your special love partner, sacrifice your own inferior self to win them over, and hold on to them forever.

Is it any accident that we use the expression "falling in love" to describe this romantic insanity? It is an all-consuming descent into passion and compulsion. We drown in love. We fantasize about our lover constantly; we can think of little else. It is far from elevating. No one "rises" in love. We tumble into it without much thought or choice, much as we might stumble into an open manhole. The falling part is easy; climbing back out again . . . not so much.

Whenever we consider another person special and decide that we need them to fulfill us, we affirm that we are incomplete—that we are lacking in some vital way. But God cannot lack, nor can God's creation. We were created whole, and whole we remain, even though we dream we're separate. Therefore any belief in lack will keep the separation real *for us*—in our minds—and keep the awareness of God and His love at a distance.

The Secret Bargain

The special love relationship can be understood as a secret, unconscious bargain made between two flawed and incomplete beings. Neither feels whole. Both are seeking for completion, because they have forgotten their true identity as Christ or Ever-Mind. And so they come together, joining forces in the hope that each can compensate for the other's lacks. "*Each partner tries to sacrifice the self he does not want for one he thinks he would prefer.*"[6] Such an arrangement has nothing to do with real love. It is a deal struck between two egos, a mutual-defense pact that compensates for each other's weaknesses in a frightening and dangerous world.

This alliance is shaky from the start, because if the other has what you lack and need, then you are dependent on them. You can't afford to lose them and what they provide for you. You will need to control them, to keep them close. If your attempts at control are too obvious, though, you risk driving them away. Instead you must offer them something of yours that *they* need. And you'll make certain they know about this great sacrifice you're making on their behalf. Then *they* will feel guilty. They'll owe you. Their guilt will bind them to you, and they won't ever dare leave. Of course, they do the same to you. Guilt cuts both ways.

If this guilt is strong enough, the secret bargain you've struck together will hold. Neither will abandon the other or dare to reveal the other's weaknesses to the world for fear of being exposed themselves. But such an arrangement is anathema to intimacy. Like the bargain itself, the guilt must remain hidden. Neither partner wants transparency, because neither wants to look honestly at their dependency and what it says about them. Nor can they risk being truly *seen* by the other. To expose their secret flaws would make them too vulnerable. Their partner might realize just how damaged they are and decide to move on. If intimacy joins us together, the secret bargain preserves distance under the cover of false union.

Remember too that bargains can only be struck within the world of separation. They require two parties with different agendas coming together out of mutual interest. They are not about love or union. "*[The ego] is always willing to strike a bargain, but it cannot understand that to . . .*

gain you must give, not bargain. To bargain is to limit giving, and this is not God's Will." [7]

In God's reality, the only thing that can be given is love, and the giving and receiving are equivalent and simultaneous. Not so for the ego. The ego gives only to get, and this is not true giving. It is parasitic, not symbiotic. It elevates the welfare of the isolated part—in this case, itself—over that of the greater whole. Therefore the ego can bargain, it can parade its specialness, it can demand sacrifice of others and itself, and it can "fall in love"—but what it cannot do, ever, is love.

The Ego's Secret Weapon

The ego is not part of God. It is a by-product of the collective hallucination in which we believed we could separate from God. The ego was forged in the image of that separation, so separation is its currency: the only thing it understands. How, then, can it possibly know the oneness of the true Self? How can something born from separation welcome wholeness when wholeness would end its separate existence? How can something incapable of love embrace the fullness of love that is God? And could it ever view such love as anything but a threat?

To the ego, God appears deadly. Awaken to God, and the ego is no more. Therefore not only is the ego incapable of real love, it must actively oppose it. Of course it cannot do this outright or we would recognize its maneuvers and reject them, because who does not want love? It must take a different approach. Enter the special love relationship.

*   *   *

Imagine for a moment that you're the ego. Put yourself in its shoes. However much you try to pretend that you're real and important, and to convince your host of this, you know it's a ruse, a losing battle. You're doomed to fail because in fact you are *not* real. In no respect can you compete with God and God's creation. The eternal vastness of God's Love sweeps away all trace of the ego, as a tsunami carries off a particle of sand, or as pure, limitless light dispels a fleeting shadow.

What's a poor ego to do? It does the only thing it knows how to do. It cannot triumph over God and Love, but it can misdirect. It is a master of subterfuge. And so it sets about to confuse, distract, and divert you from remembering the magnificence of your true Self. It throws obstacles in your path, like pain, illness, and infirmity. It leads you down paths that promise happiness in the guise of fame, fortune, power, and bodily pleasure—alluring paths that never quite deliver what they promised. Yet despite the ego's many ruses, it's forced to contend with the unceasing appeal of love.

The call of God's Love is powerful. Even here in the ego's world of illusion, love calls out and we respond. It draws us toward union. It coaxes us toward the recognition of our shared purpose, because the one thing we all want is love. So what's an ego to do?

The ego reasons thus: *You want love? I'll give you love. But it will be* my *brand of love. You'll find it so tempting that the moment you get a taste of it, you'll lose all interest in God's love. If I can convince you that my idea of love is what you really desire, that it's the key to your happiness; if I dangle it in front of you constantly, but just out of reach, such that you're always chasing after it—then you might never notice the powerful, unceasing attraction of God's Love.*

The ego pulls a bait and switch. It takes specialness, dresses it up in the guise of love, and parades it before us in an endless variety of potential love partners: tall, short, blond, brunette, skinny, muscular, curvy, independent, needy, smart, crafty, plainspoken, accomplished, sincere, intimidating. Each body, each personality, is endowed with its own unique set of characteristics, its own secret history of hurts and desires, its own urgent need for someone special who will save it from having to face the fact that it stands alone, separate from oneness and all creation.

This infinite variety can keep us searching for a lifetime—or many lifetimes. Yet even when we find "the one" we think we're looking for, the perfect match who'll "complete" us, we're still quietly dissatisfied. Sure, they're absolutely wonderful. But they'd be even more wonderful if only they had a bit more of this or that quality, if only they were more like someone else, if only . . . they were perfect.

We idolize our special love partners. We want them to bring us perfect love in a world of imperfection, a world specifically designed to hide love from us. Of course they fail. Perfect love does not exist in a world dreaming of separation from God. The source of true perfection is not found outside us. No human being can deliver it. As we've seen, it exists only within. That's where we must seek it. When we find it, we will no longer desire specialness. Our relationships will be based on wholeness and holiness instead.

The Course makes this point in particularly stark language in the following passage, which details the difference between the special (or unholy) relationship and one based in holiness.

An unholy relationship is based on differences, where each one thinks the other has what he has not. They come together, each to complete himself and rob the other. They stay until they think that there is nothing left to steal, and then move on. And so they wander through a world of strangers, unlike themselves, living with their bodies perhaps under a common roof that shelters neither; in the same room and yet a world apart.

A holy relationship starts from a different premise. Each one has looked within and seen no lack. Accepting his completion, he would extend it by joining with another, whole as himself. He sees no difference between these selves, for differences are only of the body. Therefore, he looks on nothing he would take.[8]

When we see no lack in ourselves or others, when we know we are complete because we were created that way by God, we will want nothing from our sisters and brothers that they cannot deliver. Because the only thing we will want is love.

4

The Roots of Dependency

In the special relationship, dependency is confused with love. The enduring appeal of popular song lyrics testifies to this truth: *Baby, I need your lovin'. Without you, babe, what good am I? Since you left me, honey, I'm no good.* In the popular imagination, if we're not feeling this kind of mutual dependency, then we must not be in love.

Where does such dependency come from? What are its origins? And why does it feel so much like love? If it's so widespread, so ingrained that it's been a staple of popular culture since at least Shakespeare's time, there must be some powerful need in us that drives it.

There is a time in our lives when this sort of dependency is quite natural. As infants, we had to depend on adult caretakers for our very survival. If they abandoned us, we really would die. In this we had no choice. We had to trust that they loved us enough to provide for our needs and never leave us.

Every human being begins life from this position of ultimate dependency. Although it's impossible to consciously remember what this felt like, its remnants persist in the special love relationship. If we revisit those lyrics from popular music and hear them in this context, they take on a whole new meaning: *I can't make it without you. Please, please don't leave me! I need you and only you, my one perfect love.* The helpless infant, the powerless child still live within each of us. We may grow around them, fashioning new, more competent identities for ourselves, but from deep inside they still cry out. They find their most plaintive and persuasive voice in the special love relationship.

If your basic needs as an infant were left unmet, then naturally you will enter relationships later in life from a position of lack. You will *expect* to be deprived, ignored, and abandoned. These feelings will be triggered even by your partner's most insignificant lapses. Each time they disappoint you, each time your expectations go unmet, you will reexperience that childhood fear of abandonment with full force.

You may blame your partner, but deep down you're certain that some fundamental flaw in your nature makes you unlovable. Why else would your parents have treated you poorly? As a child you could not have understood the reasons behind their failure, but it is inconceivable that you'd have blamed them for it. You needed them too much. In order to maintain some sense of predictability over life, *their* failure had to become *yours.* Because if the problem lies with you, then at least you have a chance of fixing it someday and making it possible for them—or someone like them—to love you. If you know that your parents did not love you; if they loved you sometimes, but not consistently; or if they loved you, but for some reason were unable to properly care for you, then your goal in the special love relationship is to replay that drama and give it a better ending.

Certainly this is true for many people. But is it universal? Are we *all* victims of inadequate parenting? Could that be possible?

Consider this hypothetical situation. Assume that your parents *were* perfect—able to anticipate and respond to your every need. You lacked for nothing, certainly not for love. If your earliest years were a nonstop slide show filled with highlights of happiness and joy, would you still crave a special relationship? Would you still need someone to complete you? Would you still hunger to meet your soul mate?

These are not rhetorical questions; they are trick questions. Because who on earth can possibly claim to have had such a childhood? What parent manages to fulfill their child's every need? Parents screw up. Even if they didn't, growing up inevitably inflicts hurts like being teased and ostracized by peers that the love of a parent can no longer solace. Adolescence is a battleground. We limp our way through it. And by some strange coincidence, this is the time when special love exerts its most powerful appeal.

In the special love relationship, we play out with our partners (real or fantasized) the wounds and dependency of childhood. We look to them for the love and acceptance we once sought from mom and dad. This is true regardless of how good they were as parents.

In the special relationship, we act out a substitution fantasy. We stage a makeover of childhood, casting our special partner in the role once played by our parents. *He* will recognize our unique value—as our parents did not; *she* will never pull back the curtain and expose our insecurities—as our parents did. The special relationship is an attempt to balm the wounds incurred in childhood and abolish the guilt and shame of the past. My partner's special love will heal me. Inevitably that strategy must fail, however, because no amount of special love can compensate for the hurts of the past.

If things didn't work out in childhood, when your needs were far simpler and your parents were in a much better position to fulfill them, why ever would you expect things to be different this time around, when you want so much more and are asking it of someone who, like you, is flawed and ill-suited to provide it? Special love does not balm wounds. It inflames them. It pushes the rawness and hurt of childhood forward into the present day, where it confirms the belief that you are lacking and unworthy of ever being loved.

The True Source of Lack

The fact that growing up is so universally challenging says a lot about the ego and its world. No matter how loving your parents and family were, you will at some point meet with hardship, failure, and loss. You will be hurt physically and emotionally, and some of those hurts will scar you for life. That's not your parents' fault.

There is no perfect parent, just as there is no perfect child. It's unreasonable, and unhelpful, to hold parents responsible for our attraction to special love. We've all been held hostage by that impulse. The conviction that we are lacking, which drives the need for specialness, must have its source elsewhere.

*   *   *

If you are a being of perfect oneness, created by a Being of perfect oneness, there is nothing that you can lack. You *have* everything because you *are* everything. Only oneness exists, without aspects or parts, so what could be lacking?

However, the moment you diverge from oneness and become something else, lack is possible. You no longer have everything. Oneness appears to have abandoned you. In fact, having lost your identity as *everything,* you are left with nothing, or so it seems. The abandonment feels total. The mind is fractured. Differences, judgments, comparisons, and preferences are now not only possible but inescapable. What does this new "I" want and what does it *not* want? Who or what will serve it better?

Ideally it wants to return to oneness, but it no longer remembers the way back. Furthermore, this new "I" has its own agenda. It disdains oneness, because it knows it can never achieve it. It wants something *better* than oneness, something more special than love, something that will justify its decision to separate. This "I," this new self, is of course the ego.

If you really were an ego and nothing else, there would be no hope of ever returning to oneness. But that's not the case. You can't change the nature of what God created you to be. You can only *dream* that you've changed, and in that dream believe you've become something else, something you're not and could never be. As long as you stay asleep, you will believe your dream is real. Your dream of separation makes the ego real *for you*.

This places you in a bind. You love this ego that you made. Part of you wants to keep it alive because you made it. But you also know deep down that the ego is not you and that this world is not your home and never will be. Even so, you do long for home, so your mind splits. One aspect knows the truth and remembers the wholeness it never left. The other has swallowed the poisonous fruit of separation and now believes itself to be an individual body containing a private mind. Which is your real self? Which do you choose? Your allegiance is split. You want it both ways. But they are incompatible, and eventually choose you must.

The ego tries to solve your dilemma by offering you a compromise, a fiction of wholeness, through the special love relationship. You can stay broken in pieces and still experience wholeness, the ego promises, if you just find the perfect partner, the one who completes you. And so the search begins—not for God, not for wholeness, but for a substitute: a facsimile of wholeness that will keep you pacified and dreaming the ego's dream.

The wound from which we all suffer—the wound that fuels the special love relationship—does not come from our parents or any other human being. It is self-inflicted. It is a split in the Self that leaves us feeling incomplete because we *are* now incomplete. Instead of admitting this and seeking to return to wholeness, however, we hunt for a special partner.

In a sense, the needs we project onto our lover in the special relationship do indeed have their origins in poor parenting. But it's not the parenting we received as children. The real "poor parenting" comes from asking the ego to parent and watch over us instead of God. This primal sense of lack, and our attempts to compensate for it, comes to define us and drives our desire for specialness. It's what we believe about ourselves, and what we believe everyone else feels as well. "*Everyone makes an ego or a self for himself. . . . He also makes an ego for everyone else he perceives.*"[1] These egos stumble about like blind creatures in the night, fumbling to grab hold of someone—anyone—to steady themselves and keep from falling, not realizing that those they grasp are as blind and unstable as they are. They try to make sense of where they are and learn how to get about safely in the darkness, never understanding that what they really need is to *see*.

Managing Attraction

You might think of the special love relationship as a dream within a dream: a dream of special love within the greater dream of separation and lack of love, a dream of restitution for the loss of God. One dream tries to offset the other and make it tolerable or even desirable. No wonder, then, that special love is so compelling.

I began studying *A Course in Miracles* intensively when I was twenty. By the time I was twenty-five, I felt I knew it very well. I had read all about the special love relationship and the mutual sacrifice it involved. I knew it was a diversion from God's plan for salvation. I had already had a direct mystical experience of God—what the Course calls "revelation"—that was beyond anything the world could offer. But the lure of special love is so strong that none of this mattered. I still desired special love, and nothing could stop me from chasing after it.

Looking back, had I decided at that time in my life to avoid relationships that tempted me with specialness, I would have become a very slow learner. Why? Because for all but a very few of us, the way to handle specialness is not to try to banish it. If you feel attracted to someone, you feel attracted. Trying to deny it will merely add another layer of subterfuge. Better to accept what you're feeling and give it to the Holy Spirit to use for His purpose.

I've observed seasoned Course students twisting themselves in knots in the attempt to sanitize their desire for special love by cloaking it in the garb of holiness. One student put up a social-media post shilling for free and open group sex because, after all, God's love is equal and the same for everyone, so shouldn't we be expressing that physically? But you can't dress up special love and make it holy. It's more honest, and helpful, to dive in and let those powerful feelings play out. Notice where your fantasies lead you. Let them collide with the impossibility of two separate individuals finding their way to union through specialness. Eventually, after enough attempts and given enough pain, we'll realize that specialness can't get us anything that's real or lasting. It's not what we want. The truth is, we don't know what we want.

When I was younger, I craved relationships that didn't work out, leaving me devastated. With the benefit of hindsight, I thank God they didn't. They would have been a mess. More importantly, they would have sidetracked me for years. They would have gotten in the way of other relationships that may have been less attractive to my ego at the time, but which turned out to deliver far more in the way of love, growth, and learning.

So what should we as Course students do when we feel attracted to someone? Recognize that, like everything in the ego's world, we don't know what that feeling of attraction really means. We don't know what it's for. We're too lost in dreaming. Whenever we feel a strong desire for *anything*—a person, an object, or an outcome—it should serve as a red flag that the ego has hijacked the mind into serving its agenda.

> *Everything the ego tells you that you need will hurt you. For although the ego urges you again and again to get, it leaves you nothing. . . . Where the ego sees salvation it sees separation, and so you lose whatever you have gotten in its name. Therefore ask not of yourself what you need, for you do not know, and your advice to yourself will hurt you. For what you think you need will merely serve to tighten up your world against the light.*[2]

When you feel a strong attraction, when you yearn to be with that particular someone, the best thing you can do is to give your feelings, your fantasies, and your plans to the Holy Spirit, Who will use them only for the purpose of healing.

"The Holy Spirit would not deprive you of your special relation-ships, but would transform them. . . . He will restore to them the function given them by God."[3]

Ask for His help. Follow the guidance you receive, whether that comes in the form of an inner voice, an image, a feeling of peace, or a message couched in the lyrics of a song or in some seemingly random snatch of conversation you overhear. Trust that the Holy Spirit knows far better than you do what will make you happy. If it's happiness you want, you have to let go of what *you* think should happen and allow Him to lead you.

> *Only the Holy Spirit knows what you need. For He will give you all things that do not block the way to light. And what else could you need? In time, He gives you all the things that you need have, and will renew them as long as you have need of them. He will take nothing from you as long as you have any need of it. And yet He knows that everything you need is temporary, and will but last until you step aside from all your needs and realize that all of them have been fulfilled. . . . Leave, then, your needs to Him. He will supply them with no emphasis at all upon them. What comes to you of Him comes safely, for He will ensure it never can become a dark spot, hidden in your mind and kept to hurt you.*[4]

I've practiced giving my attractions to the Holy Spirit in this way and watched them fade in seconds. This used to trigger a strange sense of loss and disappointment, as if I had given up something of value, but now it brings relief and gratitude. I've also been surprised when I was guided to let the relationship blossom and take on whatever form would best help me to awaken. Remember, holy relationships do not arise exclusively from the transformation of special love. They occur whenever we're willing to see someone else—anyone else—through the eyes of the Holy Spirit and recognize the holiness in them as the only thing that's real.

*   *   *

Your true Self does not live in dreams. It remains as God created it, complete and whole. Therefore you are in need of nothing from anyone, because in God's reality there *is* no one else outside of you. We are all one. Because you do not yet recognize this truth, you keep searching. Yet your only real need *is* to recognize it.

Beneath the attraction of the special love relationship lies the honest desire for union with the goal of healing the separation. We want to join with others and lose our solitary sense of self in a greater purpose. The ego deflects this natural movement toward oneness into a twoness that falsely masquerades as union, because the two can never really become one. They can only join together to recognize they already *are* one. As long as they believe they are bodies, different and apart, they will relate to each other that way. "*For relationships, to the ego, mean only that bodies are together.*"[5] Those bodies will pursue separate agendas, because each believes it needs something different for itself, something that will make it special and better—its substitute for love and union. As a result, they can never truly join.

In dreams, no two can share the same intent. To each, the hero of the dream is different; the outcome wanted not the same for both. Loser and gainer merely shift about in changing patterns, as the ratio of gain to loss and loss to gain takes on a different aspect or another form. . . . Minds cannot unite in dreams. They merely bargain.[6]

And so each one continues to dream the dream of specialness, unaware of the one love that awaits them should they ever choose to awaken.

5

Shame and the Ego

It is remarkable how much power we have invested in the special love relationship and all it seems to promise. From our early teens until well into our senior years, we are held hostage by this desire for special love. If you're single and alone, you look for it everywhere. If you're in a relationship, you expect it from your partner continually and complain bitterly when you feel shortchanged. But as we have seen, special love is essentially parasitic. Each takes from the other in the belief that what's gained will outweigh the sacrifice of what must be given up.

The roots of the special love relationship go back to the separation, but not one person alive can remember this because it occurred so long ago—even before time began.* It took place at the level of the collective mind, not of the indi-

---

* The separation marked the start of linear time as we know it. Before it occurred, there was only eternity and after it has passed there will be only eternity. And in eternity of course there is no such thing as "before" or "after."

vidual self. The one Son of God—our true Self—seemed to fracture into the multiplicity of separate minds and bodies that we now experience as reality.* Each of us carries within a felt impression of the enormity of that split—the impossible guilt of believing we had rejected God and the terrible shame over what we thought we had become. But because we do not consciously remember this, trying to link the separation to our sense of lack may be useful in theory, but not necessarily helpful in practice. Instead we must look for its traces as they show up in our lives. We find them in the emotion known as *shame*. Only when we're able to identify shame in its many guises will we begin to address our fundamental sense of lack and free ourselves from it.

Shame versus Guilt

A Course in Miracles tells us that one of the first consequences of believing that we separated from God was guilt. We rejected God. We did something terrible and felt guilty about it. The Course has a great deal to say about this guilt. The words "guilt" and "guilty" appear almost six hundred times. By contrast, "shame" merits a mere five mentions. There is a reason for this discrepancy, and it involves the historical timing of when the Course was scribed by Helen Schucman and Bill Thetford.

Helen and Bill were research psychologists at the Columbia College of Physicians and Surgeons in Manhat-

---

* For a more complete explanation, see chapter 5 of *From Never-Mind to Ever-Mind*.

tan from the late 1950s through the mid-1970s. During that period, Freudian psychoanalytic theory dominated psychiatry. Helen and Bill were well-versed in it. Therefore it's understandable that the Course would make ample use of psychoanalytic concepts such as projection, denial, and dissociation to explain how our mind became split. In fact, the Course could not have been written before Freud, because the concepts necessary to convey its ideas had not yet been developed.

The flip side of this is that the Course could not have incorporated psychological concepts that had not yet come into being, any more than it could have anticipated cultural developments such as smartphones and social media. The concept of shame falls into this category. By the mid-1970s, when the Course was first published, there were thousands of psychoanalytic papers on guilt, but a mere handful on shame. It simply wasn't recognized as the force we now know it to be. That would not come until the 1980s.

To most of us, guilt and shame seem quite similar. Both make us feel bad. But guilt is about *something we did*, while shame is about *who or what we are*. Guilt arises in response to an action we took that we regret, while shame results from anything that exposes us as inferior, incompetent, damaged, or disgusting.

For example, a child sneaks into the kitchen and eats the last remaining chocolate-chip cookie from the batch her mother baked that morning. She knows her mother was saving that cookie for her dad. When mother catches her, the child feels guilty for having eaten the cookie. When her mother scolds her for being a selfish, inconsiderate child, however, she feels shame. That's not how she wants her mother to think of her. That's not how she wants to be seen. Guilt pushes us to accept responsibility for our misdeeds, and it can be expiated. Shame is about the condition of the self. As such, it can either be exposed or hidden.

The separation from God produced both guilt and shame in equal measure. We *did* something we deeply regretted when in our mind we broke away from God. As a result, we experienced guilt. But simultaneously we *became*, or thought we became, something inferior. If God created us as the perfect extension of His Being, which is all-encompassing love, then our belief that we could separate from Him stripped us of that majestic Identity and replaced it with one far more tenuous and inferior: the ego.

The cascade of shame did not stop with the formation of the ego. The ego could not tolerate the shameful truth behind its existence. To escape, it made the physical body—a place where it could hide and distance itself even further from the guilt and shame of its "sinful" rebellion against God. "*The body is the symbol of the ego, as the ego is the symbol of the separation.*"[1] Now the mind, with all its dark secrets, appears to be private, hidden away inside a body. The body becomes a stand-in for the self: our avatar in the virtual-reality game of life. We believe we *are* the body. It is our home and our protection. Everywhere we look, we see bodies, not minds, and no two bodies are identical. If we are bodies, as the ego insists, and if each body is unique, we cannot be equals. One must be superior and the other inferior. Herein lies the birth of shame. But shame, like the ego, will never show its true face. It hides.

*Here is the one emotion that you made, whatever it may
seem to be. This is the emotion of secrecy, of private thoughts
and of the body. This is the one emotion that opposes love,
and always leads to sight of differences and loss of sameness.
Here is the one emotion that keeps you blind, dependent on
the self you think you made to lead you through the world
it made for you.*[2]

The shame felt by the separated self permeates every
aspect of the ego's world, but it is perhaps most apparent in
our attitudes toward the physical body.

Shame Incarnate:
Varieties of Bodily Experience

It is a given in this world that you are born into a body. It is
also a fact that your body, like everyone else's, begins life as
a small, helpless infant. You cannot feed yourself. You cannot soothe yourself. You cannot communicate your needs;
you will lie there in your own feces until someone notices
that you are crying and comes to clean you up. Nor can
you control this body and its movements. The simple act of
navigating your fingers into your mouth requires months
of frustrating practice.

There is no shame in this fact, because it is universal.
Without exception, we all start life from the same helpless posture. Moreover, as an infant you are not yet aware
of your insufficiencies. Your senses have not yet developed
to the point where they can distinguish other people, and
your body-based self-concept is unformed.

This state does not last long. Anyone who's raised a child can attest to the phenomenal growth that takes place in the first year of life. At a certain point, you become aware of other bodies and the people they represent—parents, siblings, caretakers, and anyone else you come in contact with. These beings are far superior to you. They might as well be superheroes. They can move about with incredible speed and precision. They can lift you and gently rock you to sleep or pluck you from sleep and shake you in fury. Your size, strength, and abilities are no match for theirs. You are inferior—no question about it. This inferiority is the first hint of shame to come. When we criticize someone for behaving "like a baby," we are shaming them by reminding them of these qualities: helplessness, dependency, and weakness.

Your sense of shame increases as you mature and begin to interact with peers. Some are bigger than you. Others can walk or talk with more skill. You can't help but compare yourself and come out lacking. Even if you're the most advanced three-year-old on the planet, the moment you find yourself playing with a bunch of four-year-olds, you're in trouble. Whatever pride you felt in your newfound abilities will come crashing down.

The body becomes a source of shame when it smells bad and does disgusting things that are beyond your control, like farting or vomiting. Worse still, you're now expected to be able to control your body. You no longer poop into a diaper that someone else will change for you; you must get to the toilet. Any lapse in these abilities brings on terrible shame, as any child who wets their bed after a certain age will attest.

The school years are rife with shame. Kids can be relentlessly cruel in teasing their classmates over bodily features that deviate from what's considered normal: big noses, frizzy hair, freckles, scars, the way you walk or run, eyeglasses, and so on. As you grow older, your manner of dress can become a powerful magnet for shame—a commentary on both your sense of style and your social status.

On the athletic field, shame runs rampant. Those gifted with strength and coordination prosper, while the others fall behind. It's the nature of competition. Running a race, watching your opponent pull ahead of you no matter how hard you run, and losing badly is an experience of unvarnished shame. The same goes for swinging wildly at the ball and missing or dropping an easy pass. Then there is the abject shame of being picked last for the team, knowing that your peers don't want you, that they consider you a liability and an obstacle to their desire to win.

Even if you excel at sports, you will not be immune to shame. No matter how great your talent, you will eventually encounter someone who's better than you. You will lose. You will slink away with your head bowed in shame. For even the very best athletes, defeat is inevitable. Tom Brady, Serena Williams, LeBron James—all had to contend with losing. We know the great Babe Ruth as the home-run king, but in five different years he also led the American League in strikeouts.

Another element of the school experience breeds shame that can be devastating. This is the arena of physical attraction, social acceptance, and popularity. By the time you reach high school, your body has started to change in ways that have nothing to do with strength or skill. Women's breasts grow (or fail to grow); men's voices deepen, and hair sprouts from the most unlikely and awkward places. As hormones flood the brain, you begin to experience sexual desire and attraction. Now it is paramount to be seen as physically appealing, or at least to be friends with those who are popular and attractive.

Like athletic ability, some are gifted with exceptional physical beauty, but the vast majority are not. They can only look on in envy as the good-looking boys and girls cavort with each other, knowing there is no way to compete and certain that their plainness renders them invisible to kids so popular.

However, beauty and popularity are no shield against shame. Beauty puts the focus on your appearance; popularity, on the way you conduct yourself in public. Both keep you under a constant spotlight. The slightest blemish, or one uncool remark, and you come tumbling down from your lofty perch.

In the era of social media, peer influence on shame has grown astronomically. Many today calculate their self-worth by the number of "likes" they receive on Facebook and Instagram posts. The higher the number, the more popular they are. Should they post something off-color or simply get displaced by someone with more exciting posts, the number of likes dwindles, and they will feel shame.

Shame is paralyzing. When we find ourselves in its grip, we want to disappear, to hide and never be seen again. The word we use to describe extreme shame is *mortification*—to die of shame. Better to die than be exposed for the shameful being we fear ourselves to be. We see this reflected in the number of teen suicides provoked by bullying on social media. These unfortunates were literally mortified. With no other way to cope, they did indeed die of shame.

If you are human, shame plays a major role in your life, whether or not you're willing to admit it. Do you have a physical body? If so, you are vulnerable to shame—period. Nor is shame confined to the body. You feel shame for being stupid when the teacher calls on you and you don't know the answer. You feel shame for being smart and getting teased by other kids precisely because you *do* know all the answers. You feel shame if you're poor and wear cheap hand-me-down clothes. You feel shame if you're wealthy and are seen only through the lens of your money and the privilege it buys you. Shame is an equal-opportunity employer. It is impossible to grow up without some experience of it. If you think you've managed to escape from shame, you're probably one of those most affected by it. You're simply afraid to look for it, much less deal with it.

Having studied shame for decades—in myself, my family, and my psychotherapy patients—I can vouch that not a day goes by without some interaction that provokes some form of shame. We want others to approve of us. We want to be right—about everything, always—because our judgments are so often wrong. We withhold apologies, because to apologize would be to admit we were at fault. We try to make light of the hurts we've inflicted on and received from others. Should our "sins" happen to be revealed and made public, we'll do almost anything to deny them, explain them away, or stuff them back into a dark corner of the mind where no one will ever hear of them again.

Defending against Shame

The ego has four basic strategies for coping with shame. One is hard-wired. It's the most natural response to shame, but also the most raw and undefended and therefore the least appealing. The other three are learned from experience. Some people rely primarily on only one or two, while others make use of them all. We will consider each in turn.

To be clear, what follows is *not* taken from *A Course in Miracles*. However, I've found it to be very helpful in applying the Course's principles. It is a summary of the seminal work of my psychotherapy mentor Donald L. Nathanson, MD.*

Nathanson identified four fundamental maneuvers by which we try to live with shame rather than trying to heal it. He labeled them *withdrawal, avoidance, attack-self* and *attack-other*. He pictured these as occupying the four points of a compass in which *withdrawal* and *avoidance* are paired along one axis and *attack-other* and *attack-self* along the other. He called this the "Compass of Shame."

WITHDRAWAL

Withdrawal is our most natural response to shame. It is not something we learn; it is culturally and evolutionarily programmed into us. It reflects our deep desire to disappear

---

* To learn more about Dr. Nathanson's work on shame, read his book *Shame and Pride: Affect, Sex, and the Birth of the Self* (New York: W.W. Norton, 1992), 305–77.

when we're caught in an embarrassing situation. We don't want to be seen in our shame. We don't want to be *seen* at all, by anyone; the exposure of our defective self is just too painful. We drop our gaze to the ground to avoid making eye contact with those who have witnessed our humiliation. Eventually we recover enough to poke our head back out into the world; we look around, test the waters, and if the storm has passed, emerge from hiding. In most instances, we find that people have moved on and no one much cares about what happened. We are not so much forgiven as forgotten. This we welcome as a blessed reprieve.

AVOIDANCE

Avoidance is a more complex and devious strategy. It aims to disavow the very presence of shame in order to spare us from its sting. It includes any thought or behavior that's intended to eliminate shame from our awareness. The source of that shame is never addressed; we simply detour around it. Avoidance insulates us—or in the extreme, anesthetizes us—so we don't have to feel it, at least not in the moment. We are left free to deny its existence. We can hold our heads high and ask with bafflement, "What shame? Who, *me*? What are you talking about?"

The presence of shame is in itself shameful. It is self-reinforcing. That's why we don't want anyone to witness our shame. Any defense that prevents us from feeling and displaying shame will be compelling and widely utilized.

The most common avoidance mechanism is substance abuse. Take your drug of choice, apply it liberally to those areas where you've been bruised by shame, and presto—

you feel just fine! Alcohol is notorious for alleviating shame. How else to explain the popularity of a liquid that's dangerously addictive, makes you impulsive and reckless, can make you puke, and leaves you hungover the next day? Don Nathanson used to quip that "shame is soluble in alcohol," by which he meant that it dissolves and disappears from sight, like salt sprinkled into a glass of water. With enough alcohol, the shy become the life of the party. Truths can be blurted out and confidences shared that would otherwise make us blush. As long as we're intoxicated, this release from shame feels freeing and boisterous. It can create the illusion of a wonderful bond between drinkers. But it's a false closeness; it fades rapidly as the effects of the drink wear off and sobriety returns.

Other substances have their own special charms. Cocaine envelops the user in a cloud of chemical exhilaration so dense that nothing shameful can penetrate. Cannabis offers a cloak of giggling naivete, as well as greater absorption in sensory stimuli like music or nature. This masks shame and keeps it at a comfortable distance. Opiates like heroin and fentanyl top them all. They flood the brain with a tsunami of bliss, sweeping consciousness into sweet oblivion, carrying with it all cares, threats, or injuries, as well as any sense of personal responsibility or failure.

No substance has effects that last forever. You awaken the next day to confront the same shabby self you tried to ditch staring back at you glassy-eyed from the bathroom mirror. In fact, you feel worse—more shameful—for having lost control and behaved so badly. To escape, you must line up another round, another line, another hit. And the addictive cycle continues—wash, rinse, repeat.

Nonchemical addictions serve just as well to keep shame at bay. The mental intensity and nearly total absorption of gambling, sex, binge eating, or workaholism—all will do the trick . . . for a while. But the cure for shame cannot be found in any substance or activity. In the end, they will all let you down.

Avoidance as a defense against shame is not limited to substance abuse or addiction. Other ways to disavow or minimize shame meet with greater social approval. Remember, *anything* that helps make you impervious to shame is serving the purpose of avoidance. Anything that diverts attention away from your vulnerabilities and onto other areas where you shine will work. It's a bait and switch. The most commonly used diversions involve wealth, status, sexual conquest, fame, and proofs of exceptional achievement. "Don't look at my embarrassing failures. Look over here. See how rich, smart, attractive, famous, and successful I am."

It's like the scene from *The Wizard of Oz* in which the all-powerful wizard has been revealed behind the curtain as nothing but an old con man. He tries to hide from the shame of his discovery and reassert his power by warning Dorothy and her companions, "Pay no attention to that man behind the curtain. The great and powerful Oz has spoken!" But it's too late. The truth has been exposed for all to see.

Here's how avoidance works. If you've accumulated massive amounts of money, how can you be shameful?

You're obviously superior. Your wealth buys you a permanent pardon from shame. If you have multiple advanced degrees or won prestigious awards in your field, how can you be shameful? You're too brilliant, too accomplished. If you've achieved fame or notoriety in some other area, like entertainment, sports, or politics, you are free to behave as though shame can't touch you. People see you as the persona you've so carefully crafted and not as your true self.

But when your admirers have gone home and you're left alone with yourself, the shame has a way of creeping back in. It's no wonder that so many stars and athletes have drug problems. Worse still, when your false image blows up, shame slams into you with full force. The politician, billionaire, or movie star outed for sexual abuse will withdraw and hide from sight. Their public image can no longer shield them from the deplorable things they've done. They take an abrupt "vacation" where they can't be reached for comment. Alternately, they attempt stronger avoidance maneuvers. They deny; they outright lie: "This is absurd. I would never do such a thing!" Should that fail, they resort to *attack-other* by viciously smearing their accusers.

Attack as Defense: Attack-Self

Withdrawal and *avoidance* make up one axis of the Compass of Shame. The other axis is defined by *attack-self* and *attack-other*. We rarely recognize avoidance for the defense it is, because its goal is to keep shame hidden. With the two attack defenses, however, the attempt to deflect shame is readily apparent.

Attack-self is fairly easy to understand. You feel embarrassed. You anticipate that others will notice your embarrassment and think less of you for it. You decide to beat them to the punch by attacking yourself first. You don't try to deny your shame; you bring it forward and make a show of it, poking fun at yourself, hoping to forestall criticism and retain some control over how others perceive you.

At a fancy dinner, you knock over a glass of red wine and it spills all over the white tablecloth. "What a klutz I am!" you proclaim. Perhaps you expect to be criticized, or you simply feel shame over your clumsiness. Either way, you deal with it through *attack-self.* You're willing to inflict shame on yourself in order to minimize its intensity and prevent others from shaming you further. After all, once you own your mistake, it becomes much harder for anyone else to criticize you. They're more likely to empathize and pardon your behavior with a good-natured quip.

This open acknowledgment of shame leads to a sense of relief for everyone present: both the shamed and the witnesses to that shame. There's a commonality and bonding in it. By employing *attack-self,* the shamed party spares everyone from having to bear witness to their shame and vicariously participate in it. After all, it could have been them. This is why *attack-self* is such a staple of stand-up comic routines. The comedian exposes her own foibles with humor, knowing that the audience members have all felt the same way at some time. Everyone laughs from the release of tension. The comedian serves as a conduit for this communal shame: a self-appointed scapegoat. She finds absolution and even pride when the audience goes wild with applause.

Attack-self can be used effectively in more troubling situations as well. I once treated a woman in her thirties who'd suffered a massive bleed into her brain. Fortunately, she survived without any permanent harm, but her head had been shaved for surgery, and as her hair grew back, it was no longer jet-black; it came in gray. This was a source of terrible shame for her. She'd run into colleagues who hadn't heard about her condition, and they'd stop and stare at her in shock. "What on earth happened?" they'd ask. She was unable to answer. The shame left her fumbling for words. Her obvious distress and inability to respond created more shame until withdrawal took over and she had to turn and walk away.

I taught her to cope with this situation by using attack-self. Whenever someone looked shocked by the change in her appearance, she would jump right in and tell them, "Yeah, I know. I had a bleed into my brain, and it literally turned my hair gray. Can you believe that?" I had her memorize the words, so she didn't have to think about what to say in the heat of the moment. The comfortable acceptance displayed by her comment and its subtle humor put the other person at ease and dispelled the threat of shame for them both.

It is important not to confuse attack-self with honest self-disclosure. With attack-self, you intentionally inflict shame on yourself to avoid even greater shame. My patient continued to feel embarrassed by her gray hair. Her use of attack-self did nothing to change that, but she now had a way of responding that prevented the shame from spiraling out of control. Although it allowed her a graceful exit, it was still a defense. The open admission of our all-too-human flaws and errors is something very different. As we shall see later, it is the road out of shame.

Attack as Defense: Attack-Other

Attack-other, unlike *attack-self,* rarely leads to an outcome where everyone feels better. It demeans and separates, but it is so common that everyone has felt its sting. Like avoidance, attack-other involves a bait and switch. But unlike avoidance, which tries to deny the presence of shame entirely, attack-other weaponizes that shame and targets it onto another person instead. By attacking someone else, you make *them* the object of shame and thereby escape it yourself—at least that's the idea. You're not the one who's inadequate, incompetent, ugly, or stupid; *they* are. Avoidance disavows the presence of shame in yourself; attack-other displaces it from you onto another person.

Imagine that my gray-haired patient, instead of making a humorous quip about her own hair, had poked fun at her colleague's hair. "Didn't you bother to shower this morning?" or "Who is your stylist? She should be shot for crimes against humanity." Such are the characteristic moves of the attack-other defense.

Attack-other shows up everywhere, from the bedroom to the boardroom, from kindergarten to Capitol Hill. Siblings squabble, and when mom demands to know who started it, they point to each other. In the corporate world, if a new product launch fails, it's the fault of the other division and its arrogant director. When a film opens to poor box-office numbers, actors blame producers, producers blame writers, and writers blame other writers, who took their original masterpiece and dumbed it down to please the producers. All finger-pointing is essentially attack-other.

The habitat in which attack-other seems to thrive most naturally, and where it achieves its most vicious levels of expression, is politics. The days of Harry Truman and "the buck stops here" are long gone. Instead we are burdened with leaders who lash out at honest critics while refusing to acknowledge their own scandalous behavior, who impugn the press for doing its job, who blame the opposition for their own policy failures, and whose only goal is self-aggrandizement. Such leaders are walking, talking, tweeting exemplars of the attack-other defense against shame.

BULLYING

Bullying has received a great deal of attention in recent years, and rightly so. Bullying is dangerous. It incites violence. It provokes suicides. And in a social-media universe where a single tweet or post can deliver a devastating blow in the privacy of your own room, bullying has become endemic. However, bullying is seldom recognized for what it is: the chronic and relentless use of attack-other to spare the self from shame. By demeaning others, the bully deflects from his or her own deep-seated fears of inadequacy—which of course they can never admit to. They also send a clear signal to others: "Don't mess with me. Don't try to make me an object of shame, because if you do, I will retaliate, and massively." In this way, bullies protect themselves from internal shame while lowering the odds that they will become the victims of another's attack.

Narcissism

Avoidance and *attack-other* can combine to form a particularly noxious brew in the condition known as *narcissism*. Viewed from the outside, you would never guess that the self-absorbed narcissist was suffering from extreme shame. Which is precisely the point. They have achieved their goal and hoodwinked you.

Narcissism is a brick-wall defense against shame. It reflects a wish to be shame-proof, to expunge shame from the mind entirely. It also serves as a powerful illustration of what happens when the ego shrugs off any pretense of caring about others and runs amok in its own self-glorification.

Narcissists makes use of avoidance by extolling their accomplishments to the point of absurdity and deceit. Truth is a secondary consideration—and a minor one at that—when it comes to the need to prop up the self-image. These individuals are the greatest in their chosen field, which is of course the only one that matters. They are the most attractive, the richest, the smartest, the most successful. So certain are they about their inestimable value that there is no use debating it with them.

Narcissism is purchased at a price. At any moment, the winds of fortune could turn, and narcissists could find themselves toppled from their perch. This is where attack-other takes the stage. Anyone who could be seen as more attractive, smarter, or more successful, that is, any potential rival, must be cut down to size. They must be attacked and shamed until they no longer pose a threat.

The narcissist teeters on a narrow pinnacle. He must stay constantly alert to such threats and attack them immediately. This helps explain the narcissist's penchant toward paranoia. Unseen forces with malevolent intent are forever out to destroy him. Conspiracies against him abound. Anyone and everyone is viewed as a potential threat. The real threat, of course, comes not from outside but from within. His paranoia is an accurate reflection of his own fear that the terrifying disowned shame he's held at bay for so long will one day leach to the surface for all to see, like toxic ooze in a Superfund cleanup site.

Psychotherapists agree that narcissism is almost impossible to treat. Why? In order to treat it, the underlying shame must be exposed and experienced. How else can its roots be traced and healed? Yet this exposure is precisely what the narcissist expends all their energy fighting against. A narcissist in a therapist's office would be like a medieval knight visiting a dermatologist for a rash and refusing to remove his suit of armor. The narcissist will try to use the therapist the same way he does everyone else—as a prop to shore up a fragile self-image that's perpetually on the brink of collapse. He will try to impress the therapist with his brilliance and regale her with tales of his accomplishments and conquests—all to prove that there is nothing he could possibly gain from therapy. In fact, he's almost certainly the most psychologically healthy, amazing human being this therapist has ever encountered, and isn't she fortunate that he chose *her*?

A wonderful saying attributed to psychologist Stephen Grosz perfectly captures the narcissist's predicament: *the bigger the front, the bigger the back.* Which is to say, the greater the need to embellish the façade and impress others, the greater the underlying rot that must be covered over and hidden from sight. Massive shame requires massive concealment.

What is the narcissist like in relationships? The simple answer is that he has no relationships—no intimate relationships in any case. The narcissist is incapable of intimacy. The last thing he wants is to be seen truly by another human being, because they would discover his dark secret shame, and that he can never allow. Therefore all of the narcissist's relationships are transactional and acquisitive. He will ally himself with others only to the extent it benefits himself. He will smile and schmooze and pretend to be loving or whatever else is required in order to get what he wants. For the narcissist, relationships have no value in themselves. They are merely a means to an end.

The Ego as Narcissist

You may wonder why a book about relationships and forgiveness in *A Course in Miracles* would delve into narcissism and its roots in shame. After all, only a very few meet the diagnostic criteria for narcissistic personality disorder, and those who do are unlikely to be reading a book on relationships. The answer is simple. To the extent that we identify with the ego and give it a home in our minds, *we are all narcissists.* The classic narcissist offers us an extreme caricature of how we see ourselves and relate to others when identified with the ego.

As we've seen, the ego suffers shame from which it can never escape, because shame is part of how it came into being. It bears the shame of knowing it is *less than*—less than God and less than your true Self, which God created. Like the narcissist, the ego must engage in a constant battle against this shame. It needs you (and everyone else) to treat it as if it were God. It feeds on the acclaim and attention of others. "*The ego tries to exploit all situations into forms of praise for itself in order to overcome its doubts.*"[3] It must prove that it is not less than, but greater than; not illusion, but reality. Failing that, it must distract us from the unvarnished realization that *it is nothing*. Because if we truly acknowledged this—if we came face-to-face with the shadowy figure behind the curtain and discovered that it was *unreal,* a sham, a stick figure inside a dream—we would discard it in a flash and awaken to truth.

To support its deception, the ego relies on all four defenses from the Compass of Shame. It *withdraws*, hiding from sight and hoping that you (and everyone else) will overlook its history of failures and give it another chance to prove itself. It *avoids* the shame of its nonexistence by sending you chasing after all manner of special shiny objects. It further avoids shame by hunkering down in the body, seeking release through food, drugs, and other addictive activities that distract the mind and lull it into complacency. Of course the ego prefers never to attack itself, but it will attack *you* if it sees advantage in it. And it certainly attacks everyone else with its relentless stream of judgments.

Like the narcissist, the ego is incapable of real relationships. It can only strike bargains and sacrifice its inferior self on the altar of another's perceived specialness. *"Egos do join together in temporary allegiance, but always for what each one can get* separately."[4] To the ego, any inclination to truly join with others in a shared purpose is terrifying. It is viewed, correctly, as a move toward oneness. This poses an existential threat. For the ego, attack is always preferable to joining, because it maintains the sense of separation.

The ego assures you that the best defense is a good offense. The only way to really protect yourself is by attacking first. But in order to attack, you must first believe that you are a body, and that everyone else is also a body. Spirit does not attack. Minds without bodies cannot attack. A mind is incapable of hurting another mind unless it operates through a body, whether that's with a critical scowl, a sarcastic comment, a sucker punch, or a knife to the throat. Therefore every attack reinforces the belief that you and the other are bodies, and in competition. However, if you are a body, your attack makes you vulnerable to counter-attack, which you must then defend against—and around and around it goes. The ego's world is a frightening battleground, where you either triumph or perish, and where even your triumphs are short-lived and destined in the end for failure.

Attack and the Ego

We saw earlier how the ego's fundamental sense of lack fuels its hunger for special relationships. It is parasitic. It wants to improve itself by taking from another. If viewed honestly, all of the ego's relationships—that is, all *special relationships*, regardless of their form—are nothing more than covert forms of attack.

When you think of the word *attack*, it might be more accurate to think *at-lack*, because without the ego's innate sense of scarcity and inferiority, attack would not be possible. This is an important point, and one with powerful repercussions. It means that the ego *must* attack because it is always "at-lack." It can never rest safely, confident in its own sufficiency. Someone or something—whether a person, fate or God Himself—is always threatening to take away its precious possessions, its money, its special relationships, or its very existence. The ego defends itself by attacking. "*When the ego experiences threat, its only decision is whether to attack now or to withdraw and attack later.*"[5] But attack it must, because it is ever at risk, ever at-lack. It's like a hungry shark that must attack and devour everything in its path that might prove its nothingness, in order to survive with its self-importance intact.

> *The strong do not attack because they see no need to do so. Before the idea of attack can enter your mind, you must have perceived yourself as weak. Because you attacked yourself [with the separation] and believed that the attack was effective, you behold yourself as weakened. No longer perceiving yourself and your brothers as equal, and regarding yourself as weaker, you attempt to "equalize" the situation you made. You use attack to do so because you believe that attack was successful in weakening you.*

> *That is why the recognition of your own invulnerability is so important to the restoration of your sanity. For if you accept your invulnerability [as the Son of God], you are recognizing that attack has no effect. . . . Therefore, by attacking you have not done anything. Once you realize this you will no longer see any sense in attack, for it manifestly does not work and cannot protect you.*[6]

Whenever you are tempted to attack, or when you catch yourself in an attack thought, ask yourself the following questions:

- *In what way has this situation made me feel weak and lacking?*
- *Exactly what is it I want that I feel deprived of, and why do I want it so much that I'm willing to attack?*
- *Does this situation threaten some aspect of my self-concept that I cherish, something essential to my self-image as the ego sees it?*
- *Do I want to feel vulnerable and inferior like the ego? Or invulnerable and safe as a Child of God?*

Try to recognize the ego's attack for what it is. Dig deep to find the shame, the belief in lack, that motivates your desire to attack. Then remind yourself that your true Self is not a body or an ego. You are the mind that God created one with Him: an extension of His Mind, the Ever-Mind that lives within us all. When you affirm this, you reclaim your invulnerability and relinquish the need to attack. In its place you discover the power of your innocence.

A Course in Miracles teaches that all attack is really an attack on yourself, or rather on your Self. You may think you're directing your attack outward at others and that this is necessary and justified, but in reality you inflict damage only on yourself. "Those who live by the sword die by the sword." (We will explore this in more depth in part 2.) As Workbook lesson 126 states: *"All that I give is given to myself."* Give attack, and that is what you you'll get back.

When we attack, we are at-lack. But what exactly is it we're lacking? What do we need so badly? The ego tries to answer this but cannot. We lack union with our fellow humans, the split-off aspects of our true Self. We lack the perfect love that is the very essence of the Self. We lack the oneness we once knew with God. Of course, these all turn out to be the same thing—the fruit of our belief in the separation. *"A sense of separation from God is the only lack you really need correct."*[7] Attack does not correct separation. It exacerbates it by making it seem more real.

> *When you attack, you are denying yourself. You are specifically teaching yourself that you are not what you are. . . . If you understand that this is always an attack on truth, and truth is God, you will realize why it is always fearful. If you further recognize that you are part of God, you will understand why it is that you always attack yourself first.*
>
> *All attack is Self attack. It cannot be anything else. Arising from your own decision not to be what you are, it is an attack on your identification. Attack is thus the way in which your identification is lost, because when you attack, you must have forgotten what you are.*[8]

When we remember our true Self and see its reflection shining from the faces of our brothers and sisters, attack will have no meaning. In fact, it will become impossible. We will lack for nothing—nothing real, that is. Therefore *shame will no longer exist*. In the midst of oneness, all notions of more or less, superior or inferior, mine or yours, become nonsensical. We are complete in God, and any memory of lack, shame, or attack will have dissolved back into the nothingness from which it appeared to have come.

6

Healing Shame, Escaping Ego

As a psychotherapist, I have sat with hundreds of people afflicted with the wounds of guilt and shame. They had good reason to feel the way they did—or so they believed. One young man was convinced that his arms were too skinny. He hid them by wearing long-sleeved shirts even in the heat of summer. He worked out vigorously; his bulging biceps were a testament to his efforts, but to no avail. His shame overcame his attempts to conquer it, and he remained obsessed with and embarrassed by his "skinny" arms.

A woman felt she was undeserving of love because of the abuse she'd suffered as a child. If her own mother and father could treat her so badly, she reasoned, there must be something very wrong with her.

A Catholic widow in her seventies was "ordered" into treatment by her parish priest. He'd grown tired of her compulsive need to confess and seek absolution every single day for a brief affair she'd had over thirty years earlier.

A bright young woman performed amazing work for her firm, but got none of the credit because the brash, good-looking guy she reported to presented her work as his own. He got the kudos—and the promotion.

A middle-aged woman suffered from a chronic pain condition that prevented her from socializing. She'd lost all her friends as a result. Her isolation and shame were almost as debilitating as her pain.

Again and again I have heard such stories. Guilt about a hurtful action festers into chronic shame. Shame, borne over a lifetime, leads to failures that result in guilt. Round and round these cycle, feeding into each other, seemingly with no way out. My job as a psychotherapist was to listen to my patients' tales and offer them a different narrative, a new way of understanding what had happened that could help free them from their prison of guilt and shame. In psychotherapy such a reinterpretation is called a *reframe*.

Reframing Shame

A reframe is a new way of understanding the incident that incited so much guilt and shame. If the story were pictured in a painting (say of a bleak landscape), we would be placing it in a new frame, one that doesn't change the picture, but brings forward different colors and aspects of the scene to make it more inviting.

As an example, I once treated a young man we'll call Rick, who was racked with guilt and shame over an incident from his adolescence two decades earlier. When Rick was thirteen, his older sister had seduced him, and he held himself responsible. I suggested three reframes—alternate ways of viewing his behavior, as well as his sister's—that would allow him to release the profound guilt and shame he'd carried as part of his self-image. First, I pointed out that at thirteen years of age, with hormones raging, it's a rare male who can resist a come-on from an interested older woman. He was holding his younger self to a very high standard. We then explored the motives for his sister's seduction within the context of their family. Their parents had been emotionally distant and uninvolved with both children, pretty much leaving them to fend for themselves. Third, I reminded him that he had remained faithful to his own wife although he had been approached sexually by female coworkers on a number of occasions.

Each of these reframes highlighted information that was not entirely new to Rick. He could have observed these things on his own. But his crushing shame and guilt had so filled his mind that it crowded out the possibility of finding other, kinder ways of interpreting his and his sister's behavior. My reframes offered him different perspectives. Maybe he was not a sexual predator after all, as he feared, but just a fairly typical adolescent male. His sister's seduction was less about him than about her need for love and attention from their absent parents, a need both children felt. And Rick had responded to his inability to resist her by determining never to repeat his lapse and succumb to sexual temptation again. He had taken this upsetting event from his past and used it as a bulwark against future temptation—successfully! That was something to be proud of. Given these reframes, when Rick thought back on the incest now, instead of being flooded with shame, he could see the bigger picture and forgive himself. Equally importantly, he could forgive his sister.

Rick had been held hostage by feelings that belonged to that troubled era from his past. They did not really fit with his present-day self. My reframes enlarged the context within which he viewed his behavior, and as a result his judgment of himself softened. No longer was he the weak-willed victim of his manipulative sister; nor, at the other extreme, was he a sexual predator and deviant. He was a decent guy who'd struggled with his sexual impulses at a difficult time in his life and emerged with some scars. Nothing more.

Were the particular reframes I offered Rick the only ones possible? Of course not. Other therapists might have applied different frames and achieved much the same result. A psychoanalyst might have delved more deeply into Rick's early childhood and his fantasies. A cognitive therapist would have examined the nature of his thoughts and how they worked to reinforce his guilt. An evangelical counselor might have affirmed that what he did was indeed sinful, but then used it as motivation to help him find salvation in Jesus. A past-life counselor might interpret the incident with his sister as a rebalancing of their karmic debts from some previous lifetime.

Which reframe is correct? Which is most accurate? There is no answer, because any of them might or might not have proven helpful. A song, "Gee, Officer Krupke," from the 1960s musical *West Side Story* illustrates this dilemma with particular insight and wit. The members of a street gang called the Jets are toying with a local cop, Officer Krupke, trying to help him figure out why they would choose to become juvenile delinquents. In the song, depending on the viewpoint of the observer—among them a psychoanalyst, a judge, and a social worker—they are either unloved and misunderstood, psychologically disturbed, innocent victims of society's ills, or just "no damn good." In keeping with these different perspectives, what they would need in order to reform is either love and understanding, psychoanalysis, a decent job, or "a year in the pen." Yet listening to their jeering words, we know that none of these will help. They're having too much fun to change.

What allowed Rick and countless others like him to free themselves from shame and guilt rooted in the past? Why were *my* reframes effective? Perhaps I just got lucky and chose the best ones for him. Or perhaps it was the fact that I offered him multiple reframes, so that if one happened to be less convincing, the others still worked. But I don't think any of these is the answer.

A number of studies have looked at different types of psychotherapy in an attempt to determine which are most effective. What they find is troubling for the orthodox practitioner devoted solely to one particular school of therapy. The therapist's theoretical orientation does not matter. Success does not depend upon which set of reframes you happen to apply. It's about the *relationship* between the therapist and the patient. If the relationship is strong, trusting, caring (dare I say loving), the patient is likely to improve regardless of whether the therapist is a classic Freudian hunched silently beside his couch or a tough-love drug and alcohol counselor calling out the patient's reckless behavior. The relationship is the key.

The Power of Sinlessness

The Course's categorization of relationships into either special or holy is not limited to romantic partners. It applies to *all* relationships, and that includes the psychotherapy relationship. In working with Rick, yes, I had expertise and specialized skills that I put to good use, but I don't believe they were instrumental in helping him heal. Far more important was my attitude. I had learned from *A Course in Miracles* how *not* to judge. I had learned to see my brother—in this instance, Rick—apart from the "sins" of his past. I believe that's why the reframes I offered were effective.

I saw Rick as sinless in two different ways. First, with regard to the incest, I did not shame him for what had happened. I did not compound his guilt with my own judgments, nor did I try to sugarcoat or make light of his major life trauma. In my psychotherapy and in my personal life, I try to give the benefit of the doubt. I assume that everyone does the best they can, given the information and abilities available to them at the time. As an isolated, sexually naive thirteen-year-old, Rick had little information and no ability to understand or cope. He and his sister were both responding to their difficult family environment. To my mind, he was blameless. He had made a mistake, sure. If he could get a do-over knowing what he knows now, he would make a different decision. But there are no do-overs, only *re-visions*. We can't relive the past, but we can choose to *view* it differently. As the Course reminds us, mistakes are not the same as sins. Mistakes are correctable. We make them every day. Sin, on the other hand, is permanent, indelible, a stain on the soul that can never be scrubbed out.

Without the ego, the idea of sin could not exist. In its harsh judgment, we are all damned for having left God. We are also told that we can't return, because God despises us for rejecting Him and would never take us back: we deserve both a life sentence and the death penalty. With the ego, that's exactly what we get.

So with regard to the incest, Rick had committed no sin, as I saw it. But I also saw Rick as sinless in a different sense and from a higher level. No matter what he had done or might do in the future—whether he turned out to be St. Francis or Charles Manson—he remained part of the Christ mind, the Son of God. As such, *nothing* he did within the dream mattered, *because it's just a dream*. He remained as God created him—spirit, love, a holy being—just like me. At that level we were identical.

From the perspective of wholeness, sin of any kind becomes impossible. The separated ego that self-identified as Rick may be saddled with guilt and shame over incest from years ago, but that's not the real Rick. That's not the Son of God. As a Course student, it's my job to see him *as he is*, not as he *thinks* he is. The role I played as a therapist was akin to fitting a broken leg with a cast. Rick's self-image was fractured. I held the truth about him intact in my own mind until he was able to absorb it for himself and make it his truth too—to whatever extent possible.

He was not yet ready to embrace the holiness of his reality as the Son of God. Few of us are. But he was more than ready to accept my re-vision of him, expressed through my reframes, and give up the all-consuming guilt and shame he'd carried for so many years.

This vision of sinlessness is the ultimate reframe. However, as separated beings we cannot really get to it, much less hold onto it, on our own. We live in a world defined by separation, not by wholeness. Only the Holy Spirit knows wholeness, and He can show us the way if we let Him. He will lead us to this vision of sinlessness, or rather, we can borrow His sight until we trust it enough to make it our own.

The Ultimate Reframe

The Holy Spirit sees only the truth in any situation. He does not see the past, because that's over. More to the point, it's part of the dream. As far as truth is concerned, the past never existed in the first place. And absent the past, the present moment is set free. It opens out in perfect shimmering purity into what the Course calls *the holy instant.*

> *The holy instant is the Holy Spirit's most useful learning device for teaching you love's meaning. For its purpose is to suspend judgment entirely. Judgment always rests on the past, for past experience is the basis on which you judge. Judgment becomes impossible without the past, for without it you do not understand anything.*[1]

> *God knows you* now. *He remembers nothing, having always known you exactly as He knows you now. The holy instant reflects His knowing by bringing all perception out of the past, thus removing the frame of reference you have built by which to judge your brothers. Once this is gone, the Holy Spirit substitutes His frame of reference for it. His frame of reference is simply God.*[2]

We apply countless frames of reference—countless reframes, one upon another—in a futile attempt to make sense of our lives, our relationships, and our world. All are based on the past. And so they all must be flawed, because they exclude what God knows us to be. Reality is defined by God, not by the ego. Therefore the only reframe that's universally healing, at all times and in all circumstances, is the Holy Spirit's because it's based not on the past but the *now. That's where God exists.* Everything else is illusion. Every situation, relationship, or behavior can be placed within the Holy Spirit's ultimate reframe to reveal its true nature—that it is out of step with God, and therefore it is unreal. It never happened. It is but an echo of the separation. You are set free from it. It no longer stands in the way of awakening to your true Self.

*   *   *

Following from Rick's example, we see now that the true task of the therapist is not to make an accurate diagnosis and apply specific treatment techniques in order to fix what's judged as broken. Rather, the therapist's task is to see only sinlessness in the patient. That's the task facing each of us as well in every relationship we have. The Course tells us, "*Everyone is both patient and therapist in every relationship in which he enters.*"[3] And also that "*the Holy Spirit uses special relationships, which you have chosen to support the ego, as learning experiences that point to truth. Under His teaching, every relationship becomes a lesson in love.*"[4]

If you focus on the "sins" of others—the ways they've come up short in your estimation and hurt you or disappointed you—you make those "sins" real *in your own mind*. Similarly, if you put others on a pedestal in an attempt to deny their flaws—that is, if you make them special in hopes that they'll do the same for you—you surreptitiously validate the very flaws you wanted to overlook. After all, if you didn't believe they were there, you wouldn't need to cover them up through idealization.

This is the two-edged sword of specialness. You can make others special in a negative sense by highlighting their sins in order to justify your grievances, or you can make them special in a positive sense by idealizing them in order to paper over their sins. Either way you have made their "sins" real to you.

In every relationship the transformative question is: which do you choose to value, specialness or holiness? Which do you *want* to see? That is the only decision you ever need to make. The rest will follow inevitably. If you value holiness and see it in another, you will also see it in yourself. If you value specialness and see it in another—whether positive or negative—you will see it in yourself as well. You either move toward union or further separation.

Call forth in everyone only the remembrance of God, and of the Heaven that is in him. For where you would have your brother be, there will you think you are. Hear not his appeal to hell and littleness, but only his call for Heaven and greatness. Forget not that his call is yours.[5]

This is one of the Course's central messages and a cornerstone of its teaching on relationships. *What you see in your brother is what you see in yourself.* Are your brothers and sisters guilty of sin in any form? Then so are you. Are they sinless and innocent, as God created them? Then so are you.

If we are sinful, we will seek to cover up our shame so no one can see it and judge us for it. Like Adam and Eve, we'll need a fig leaf to hide behind, and that fig leaf is specialness. We will also be happily distracted by the fig leaves of others and prefer to focus on them rather than the holiness that lies beneath. On the other hand, if we are sinless, the eternal Child of God, the extension of Love itself, then we needn't do anything to prove our holiness or justify our worth in God's eyes. Holiness is our birthright and everyone else's too. In the light of oneness, there is no need for specialness. It does not and cannot exist.

Identifying the Source

A Course in Miracles states many times that if you want to resolve a problem, it is not enough to deal merely with its consequences. You must first identify its *cause* and fix the problem at that level. Otherwise you are not really addressing the problem at all, only its effects, and the problem will keep recurring in one form or another. When we discover its source and correct that, then we can state with confidence that the problem has been solved.

In medicine, it's essential to make an accurate diagnosis—to identify the true cause of the patient's symptoms—before initiating treatment. Take for example the condition known as "fever of unknown origin." The patient is running a high fever for no obvious reason. The physician can prescribe acetaminophen to bring down the patient's body temperature easily enough, but that does not get at the true cause. When the medication wears off, the fever will return. Until an accurate diagnosis is found to explain the *reason* for the fever, it cannot be treated effectively.

I once attended a presentation by a young medical resident who had spent a year working in Africa. He described how one tribe would take their drinking water from one side of a large pond while using the opposite side for urinating and defecating. The tribe experienced frequent bouts of diarrhea and abdominal pain due to contamination of the water with fecal bacteria and parasites. This young physician could have handed out antibiotics and other medications to treat the symptoms, but these were only an effect. The true cause was the tribe's attempt to use the pond for two contradictory purposes. It was their only source of drinking water, and they had to prioritize keeping it clean. He taught them how to dig latrines, and the symptoms stopped.

Along similar lines, when you feel angry, you may be tempted to strike out. Perhaps you hit a pillow, punch the wall, throw something, or scream at the kids. In the heat of the moment, this seems to offer some relief. Your pent-up anger has found an outlet. But such behavior is never a real solution. If you hate your boss but feel powerless to confront her, no amount of pounding and shouting will change the situation. You'll fill up with fresh rage again and again, no matter how many times you try to get it out of your system, because you have not addressed the actual cause of your anger.

Dealing with a problem at the level of its effects rather than its cause is a hallmark of the ego. The ego's motto is "*seek, and do* not *find*."[6] The ego doesn't *want* to solve problems, because it is itself the cause of the problem. This is true no matter what form the problem seems to take. The Course is very clear: all problems stem from one source, namely, the separation and our continuing belief in its reality.

> *A problem cannot be solved if you do not know what it is. Even if it is really solved already you will still have the problem, because you will not recognize that it has been solved. This is the situation of the world. . . . Everyone in the world seems to have his own special problems. Yet they are all the same, and must be recognized as one if the one solution that solves them all is to be accepted. . . . If you could recognize that your only problem is separation, no matter what form it takes, you could accept the answer because you would see its relevance.*[7]

So how can a mind that believes in separation go about healing separation? And would the ego, the source of the problem, ever risk exposing its role—even if that were essential to solving the problem—if that exposure was certain to bring about its demise? To prevent this from happening, the ego takes an altogether different and characteristically insane approach to problem solving. It ignores the cause and deals only with effects. To solve any problem, then, whatever its form, requires us to see the ego's misdirection for what it is, then reject it and choose a different path—that of the Holy Spirit.

> *The ego seeks to "resolve" its problems, not at their source, but where they were not made. And thus it seeks to guarantee there will be no solution. The Holy Spirit wants only to make His resolutions complete and perfect, and so He seeks and finds the source of problems where it is, and there undoes it. And with each step in His undoing is the separation more and more undone, and union brought closer.*[8]

By choosing to accept the Holy Spirit's interpretation of events—that is, the Holy Spirit's ultimate reframe, in which we never left God and therefore never sinned—we begin to solve our problems at their source. As a result, we heal not only our own personal selves, but the entire separated Sonship as well.

* * *

The ego blocks us from addressing the true source of our problems by keeping that source well-hidden. It employs all the defenses of the Compass of Shame to prevent us from facing the "original sin" of guilt and shame that lives within us as a result of the separation. But if we don't face that, we can't break free of it. Which is of course exactly what the ego wants.

This is in fact the goal of *all* psychological defense mechanisms. They are strategies for managing negative emotions like anxiety, sadness, anger, or shame without addressing their true source. Psychological defenses do not resolve problems. They provide a temporary reprieve, but at the expense of identifying the problem and dealing with it at its source. Defenses warp reality. They do not cure so much as obscure. You may feel better as a result, but the underlying problem remains unchanged. And it's likely to get worse.

If you are a smoker and develop a cough that gets worse by the week, you should probably get it checked out by a doctor. But if you fear it might be something serious, like cancer, you might employ a psychological defense to avoid hearing such bad news. You could *rationalize* the cough away and attribute it to allergies. You could *deny* it's a problem, much less that it's getting worse. You could point out that someone else had an even worse cough, and it turned out to be nothing. Or you might buy some cough syrup at the drugstore and convince yourself that you've dealt sufficiently with the problem. Maybe you have. But if not . . .

Along similar lines, if you spy a discoloration in the ceiling and conclude that it's water from a leaky roof, you will most likely take action to fix it at once. On the other hand, if you question whether it's really all that discolored; or tell yourself that that spot has been there for years and you just failed to notice it before; or rationalize that it's due to the age of the ceiling; or simply decide to ignore it completely because you don't have the money to repair it, then it will get worse. The final cost will be far greater than if you'd acknowledged the problem and fixed it right at the outset.

How do we solve the problem of the ego and its defenses against shame? How can we acknowledge the problem and work to improve it when the ego distorts our ability to see it clearly? It's like trying to brush long, straight hair in a strong wind. It's impossible. You need to find some place sheltered from the wind where you can comb it and keep it neat. Similarly, shame needs a safe, peaceful place, a refuge from the winds of judgment and opinion, in which it can be brought forth and acknowledged for what it is in order to heal.

Reveal and Release

I used to keep a small wooden figurine perched on a shelf in my office as a constant reminder of the power of shame. It was given to me by a gay couple whose relationship had been torn apart by hidden undercurrents of secrecy and lies. I helped them share their secrets and fears with each other and talk about them openly. To show their appreciation, at their final session, they gave me this figurine. Its head was bowed and tucked so tightly against its body that at first it appeared to be a solid mass: no face, just a hunched ball of shame. It was an exaggerated portrayal and a reminder that, with shame, we actually lose face. Like the wooden figurine, we become an undifferentiated mass of tangled emotion. We cannot deal with the sources of our shame because they are too paralyzing to face, much less accept and resolve.

Nonetheless, we know that if a problem is to be resolved, it must be tackled at its source. And so the first step in dealing with shame (or any other negative emotion) is to look for and identify its causes. We must be willing to push past the ego's defenses in order to be totally honest, first with ourselves, then with others. We have to admit that our psychological defenses have not served us well when it comes to shame, and therefore, however counterintuitive it may seem, however anxious it makes us feel, we will go in the opposite direction. We must find the courage to bring to light what we hid out of shame.

We have seen how necessary this is for healthy relationships. If you genuinely desire intimacy—*into-me-see*—then you have to open your inner world to your partner. They need to be able to see into all your darkest corners. Total, perfect openness may be an unrealistic or even impossible goal, but you must be *willing* to hold nothing back, to share whatever might come between you, however uncomfortable that feels. Even if you think your partner might judge you for it and leave you. You may not be able to open up immediately. It can take hours, days, even years. But there should be nothing that you *choose* to keep secret.

To be clear, this does *not* mean that you're free to blurt out anything that comes into your head. Being open does not give you license to be obnoxious. Nor is it about correcting others: "I have to be honest with you, honey, that outfit makes you look fat." No, it's about disclosing the things you've kept hidden and private to protect your false self-image with the goal of freeing yourself from that image: "I pretend to be a success, but I feel like a fraud." "I've slept with over a hundred guys." "I stole someone's idea and passed it off as my own."

Withhold even one secret from your partner, and it compounds. You wind up turning yourself inside out to preserve the secrecy, telling lies on top of more lies to maintain the cover-up and protect yourself. Your secret acts like a powerful magnet, or a black hole in astrophysics: it sucks everything around it into its emotional field until the whole relationship is at risk of being swallowed up. You know that you have closed off to your partner; they can feel it too (whether or not they say anything about it). You have erected a wall between you. Behind it your secret remains safe, but at the cost of shutting out the one you love, the one who most needs to know about it if you truly want to heal.

What is still more dangerous is that you start to believe your own lies. You've not only shut out your partner and precluded any chance of intimacy, you've shut out yourself! You no longer know yourself. "*For what you would hide is hidden from you*."[9] You can't risk that hard look in the mirror. You wind up peddling a false image to the world, which you're constantly having to patch and polish, and which you try to pass off as your genuine self.

This pattern of hiding is not just a matter for psychology. It is a central tenet of *A Course in Miracles*. Our bodies serve as our public face while our thoughts stay private—or so we like to believe. However, our private thoughts have no reality. They're like thought bubbles in the ego's lonely cartoon world. Any thought that's stamped "private," any thought we choose to withhold, reinforces our sense of separateness and blocks communication with our sisters and brothers, with God, the Holy Spirit, and the Self we all share together.

The ego of course treasures private thoughts. They're all it is capable of. It cannot share love. It can only pretend to love while going about its business, cloaking itself in layer upon layer of obfuscation and subterfuge. It can never reveal the one guilty, shameful secret that lies at the core of its existence—namely, the separation from God—because then its game would be up. You would remember God and awaken. As a result, the ego cannot be truthful about *anything*. Truth is its foe.

There is a paradox here. In order to free yourself from shame, you have to be willing to expose that shame. Your innermost self, your private thoughts, must be brought to the light. And yet, by exposing what's most raw and sensitive within you, you make yourself *more* vulnerable to shame. Take Rick, for example. What if one day he decided to tell his wife about his sister's seduction and she responded by recoiling from him in disgust? What if she could no longer bear to let him near her? That would be the end of their marriage. Even if the odds of it happening were very small, it would still be quite a risk for him to take. Easier by far to keep his past hidden.

Given this dilemma, what can you do? You *will* need to open up your innermost self in order to heal—but not to just anyone and not on a whim. You share your private thoughts and feelings *only* in circumstances where you trust you'll be safe—that when you speak aloud the secrets you've tried to bury, they will be heard, respected, and honored in the spirit in which they were shared. Unfortunately, there are few settings in this world that are truly safe. Good friends occasionally qualify, but not if they've bought into the public image you've passed off as yourself. Family members tend to be less reliable. They already know too much about you (or think they do). And too often they've played a role in your earliest shameful experiences.

By contrast, psychotherapy *is* a safe setting. Your therapist has no personal relationship with you. She is not invested in preserving your bogus self-image. She's a professional, dedicated to helping you without any preconceived assumptions. And in therapy, confidentiality is a given and backed up by law.

Another safe space where exposure is both welcomed and respected is the Twelve-Step group, pioneered by Alcoholics Anonymous, but now adapted for a host of different addictive behaviors. The group setting is safe because only first names are used and members are prohibited from revealing anything they've heard. More importantly, their identities as the world sees them have no place in the group. They're not relevant to the task at hand. It doesn't matter whether you run a billion-dollar corporation or panhandle in the streets, whether you're twenty or eighty: you are a drunk, an addict. You've struggled to keep this hidden; you've tried to conquer your addiction on your own many times and met with failure. But in this setting, there's no shame in that, because everyone else in the room has experienced the same thing. They're no different than you. In this sense, all are equal.

In this equality of imperfection, there is safety. At last it is safe to be honest about yourself. But far more, it is healing. The trappings of ego—its lies, false fronts, and cleverly crafted images—are set aside for an hour or two for the common purpose of joining together in a spirit of fellowship and honesty.

It is also possible to safely reveal your innermost self in a relationship dedicated to intimacy, not to specialness. Recall that one of the criteria for intimacy is transparency: *into-me-see*. By sharing yourself completely with your intimate partner, without reservation or hesitation, you free yourself from shame. This can take place regardless of how long you've known the person. Many marriages of fifty years never come close to true intimacy, while it's possible to stumble into it with someone you've only just met. If you both feel so comfortable that you naturally open up, you can wind up talking for hours, amazed at the kinds of things you're sharing—things you've never revealed to anyone before. You're not trying to sell them on your self-image. You're not out to impress, seduce, or manipulate. You have no agenda other than the desire to be fully known.

Not all relationships subscribe to the goal of intimacy, but the need becomes especially acute when a couple is faced with a serious crisis like an affair, bankruptcy, or the loss of a child. Unless both partners are determined to face the situation honestly by sharing their innermost feelings about it without blame or shame, the relationship is likely to fail. They must understand that a commitment to transparency is crucial if they are to survive and get past the crisis. Sadly, such commitment is rare. More often, in my experience, couples confronting situations like these split up. This turns out to be easier than the raw honesty and vulnerability required of them if they are to remain together.

You do not need the safety of psychotherapy, a Twelve-Step group, or even a loving relationship to heal from shame. Just as the Holy Spirit offers us the ultimate reframe, so too is He the ultimate safe space. Our relationship with Him is the epitome of transparency, because He already knows everything about us and loves us anyway, overlooking all that's false about us in order to help us remember what's true. For the same reason, He is better than any human therapist. We *are all ego addicts*, and the Holy Spirit can serve as the ideal therapist. Like any earthly therapist, however, He needs our participation. Healing shame is a joint venture. He can only be effective to the degree that we're willing to let Him.

> *The Holy Spirit asks of you but this; bring to Him every secret you have locked away from Him. Open every door to Him, and bid Him enter the darkness and lighten it away. At your request He enters gladly. He brings the light to darkness if you make the darkness open to Him. But what you hide He cannot look upon. . . . Bring, therefore, all your dark and secret thoughts to Him, and look upon them with Him. He holds the light, and you the darkness. They cannot coexist when both of you together look on them. His judgment must prevail, and He will give it to you as you join your perception to His.*[10]

When we bring our secrets to the Holy Spirit, we are not begging for absolution. There is no hierarchy of sins: none is greater or lesser, and all are forgivable, because *there is no such thing as sin*. In the Holy Spirit's sight, all error is equal, and equally dispensed with. Where we felt shame, inferiority, failure, and sin, He sees only love and its wholeness. When we look at our relationships with the benefit of His perspective—which is the same thing as giving them to Him for healing—they transform.

> *The quiet light in which the Holy Spirit dwells within you is merely perfect openness, in which nothing is hidden and therefore nothing is fearful. . . . There is no darkness that the light of love will not dispel, unless it is concealed from love's beneficence. What is kept apart from love cannot share its healing power, because it has been separated off and kept in darkness.*[11]

The darkness that was hidden within cannot endure when brought to His "quiet light" of "perfect oneness." This does not require any specific action on our part. It will occur regardless of what we might say or do in the outer world. It needs only our willingness. It is a decision we make—a decision for God, for healing, and for forgiveness—which begins to reverse the separation and undo the ego's tyrannical reign.

Truth cannot hide, nor can it be kept hidden, except from ourselves. Even then it is easily found. We are like children who shut our eyes tightly and then wail that we have been struck blind. All we need is to be willing to open our eyes. The moment we do, truth and light will reappear. It is in their nature to reveal themselves.

> *Love wishes to be known, completely understood and shared.*
> *It has no secrets: nothing that it would keep apart and hide.*
> *It walks in sunlight, open-eyed and calm, in smiling wel-*
> *come and in sincerity so simple and so obvious it cannot be*
> *misunderstood.*[12]

"*When you want only love you will see nothing else.*"[13] It will be there for you. And you will not be able to see anything else, because in truth, there *is* nothing else.

Were we able to reveal our flaws to God through the Holy Spirit and to do this completely and consistently, we would be healed. Having removed the blocks to the awareness of love's presence, as the Course instructs, love would stream into our awareness, and we would again remember our true Self. But we can't; we're too conflicted. Private thoughts are our default setting. We know they're not uniformly loving, so we prefer not to reveal them.

Furthermore, much of our guilt and shame is so deeply buried that we're not even aware of it. This should be brought into awareness only gradually, in keeping with our readiness to face it. Otherwise it could prove too much and trigger fear. Only the Holy Spirit is in a position to gauge our readiness and shepherd this process along.

Therefore we bring to the Holy Spirit what we can, when we're able. Think of this as a slow recalibration process, in which you gradually realign the false image of yourself with God's knowledge of what you really are. The more willing you are to accept God's picture as reality and use it as your only standard for judging both yourself and others, the closer you come to accepting it as real. Whatever seems to occur within a dream—however frightening or compelling—is still just a dream. Dream that you were murdered or that you murdered someone else, and when you awaken you don't feel guilty or scared. You feel relief! "Thank God," you say, "it was only a dream."

> *You are at home in God, dreaming of exile but perfectly capable of awakening to reality. Is it your decision to do so? You recognize from your own experience that what you see in dreams you think is real while you are asleep. Yet the instant you waken you realize that everything that seemed to happen in the dream did not happen at all. You do not think this strange, even though all the laws of what you awaken to were violated while you slept. Is it not possible that you merely shifted from one dream to another, without really waking?*[14]

Along these same lines, we might also consider the dilemma posed by the ancient Chinese sage Chuang Tzu. He told of a philosopher who awoke one day from a dream in which he was a butterfly. This shook him to the core, because forever after, he could no longer be certain about his nature. Was he was a man who'd dreamt he was a butterfly? Or was he a butterfly who dreamt he was a man—and was still dreaming it?

Fortunately, with God we escape this dilemma. When we finally, fully awaken it is not to flee one dream for another. We awaken to truth. *All* dreaming ceases, and this is salvation.

* * *

What is it like to consistently release your shame to the Holy Spirit for healing? What do you experience? You may feel a number of emotions, which all turn out to be aspects of the same thing. You experience the elation of freedom, because you no longer shoulder the burden of shame. You feel open and genuine, because you have no more need to pretend and invest energy in a false self-image. You can face others honestly and meet their shame with compassion. Their false self-images no longer threaten you, nor do they pull you back into your own false image of self. Most of all, you feel peace—pervasive, abiding peace.

Peace is the hallmark of your true Self. But this peace is not simply the absence of stress. It is not a cool glass of chardonnay after a rough day. It is not an afterglow. It is a positive force in its own right. It cannot be explained, only experienced. It is the Bible's peace "which surpasses all understanding" (Philippians 4:7, New Revised Standard Version).

In the presence of such peace, it is impossible to feel inferior or less than. Specialness has no appeal. Conflict and strife fade to stillness. You may take notice of them, but they don't stick. They affect you about as much as watching a grainy old black-and-white thriller at a drive-in theater in the middle of a bright, beautiful afternoon. The movie drones on in the background, with its muffled gunshots and shrieks, but the screen is so sun-bleached, so faded, that even if you want to, you can barely follow the storyline. Only you don't want to. It's been exposed for what it is. It's no longer real.

When we allow the Holy Spirit to free us from the ego's shame, we find peace. Peace banishes conflict—not out in the world, because the world was made for conflict—but in the mind that perceives and gives meaning to that world. When we find this inner peace, it will be reflected in all of our relationships as well. As Workbook lesson 137 states, "*When I am healed, I am not healed alone.*" We all walk the same path, and we walk it together or not at all.

7

"Bring Forth What Is within You"

In 1945 a peasant stumbled upon a cave in the desert at Nag Hammadi, Egypt. It was packed with a large number of sealed earthenware jars, which contained a library of leather-bound papyrus manuscripts dating back to the fourth century AD. Like the four Gospels of the New Testament, these texts told of the teachings of Jesus, passed down through several generations from those who purportedly heard his words firsthand. However, what Jesus says in them is radically different from what the canonical Gospels say. As scholar Elaine Pagels writes, "The 'living Jesus' of these texts speaks of illusion and enlightenment, not of sin and repentance, like the Jesus of the New Testament. Instead of coming to save us from sin, he comes as a guide who opens access to spiritual understanding. But when the disciple attains enlightenment, Jesus no longer serves as his spiritual master: the two have become equal—even identical."[1] If this strikes you as remarkably similar to *A Course in Miracles*, you are correct. (Nevertheless, these alternate gospels were available only to a small and select circle of scholars at the time of the scribing of the Course. They could not have influenced Helen Schucman or Bill Thetford in any way.)

One of the best known Nag Hammadi texts is the *Gospel of Thomas*. It consists of a collection of sayings attributed to Jesus. One of them states: "If you bring forth what is within you, what you bring forth will save you. If you do not bring forth what is within you, what you do not bring forth will destroy you."[2] This simple yet cryptic passage perfectly expresses the truth about exposing what lives within us. But what exactly does it mean by "what is within you"? What must we "bring forth"? And "bring forth" for whom? To what purpose?

Viewed in the context of the previous chapter, we can easily see how these words could apply to healing shame. If you allow the shame that you've hidden within you to surface and share it openly in a safe setting, that "bringing forth" will save you. It will free you from that source of shame and spare you further shame. This alone would be worthwhile. But the bringing forth achieves much more. It catalyzes a spiritual unfolding that eventually awakens you to your true Self—that oneness of love and peace that lives in us all: the Christ or Ever-Mind,

On the other hand, if you "do not bring forth what is within you"—if you allow your shame to fester and grow—then your failure to expose it will destroy you. As we've seen, this will lead to more shame and more hiding until there's little left about you that's genuine. You become a walking, talking façade: a bland face of happiness worn to fool the world and keep the ugly truth about you hidden from others and yourself. This falsity will contaminate all of your relationships and make intimacy—*into-me-see*—impossible, because no one is allowed to see what's hidden within. Sadly, such is the state of most relationships in the ego's world. We keep private what we fear to expose, passing up the opportunity to let it go and experience true joining.

Why is it so healing to bring forth what is within? Why is it so necessary to expose shame in order to release it?

The answer is simple. By keeping shame locked inside, you reinforce its reality for you. The past and all its hurts, regrets, insults, and embarrassments ended long ago, but in your mind they live on. Each time one of those memories resurfaces, bringing with it the burn of shame, it feels as sharp as if it had happened yesterday. Your efforts to hide it have had the opposite effect. They've made it stronger. Shame feeds on concealment.

There is no safety in hiding, because what's hidden will always strive to emerge. That becomes our constant terror. "*It is only the hidden that can terrify, not for what it is, but for its hiddenness.*"[3] The mad woman locked away in the attic shrieks for release. What are the odds that she'll regain sanity while she's kept hidden, isolated from the world and treated as a pariah?

There is a medical condition that underscores the perils of this strategy. If an infection is localized to an area where the immune system cannot fully penetrate to heal it, the body will sometimes try to wall it off to keep it from spreading. The result is an abscess: a pool of pus and decay that's been cut off from the rest of the body. Is this strategy effective? Can you live a normal life if you harbor an abscess? No. Although sequestered, the infection still remains, and it causes symptoms like pain and high fever. If left untreated, it can result in death. What is the treatment? Antibiotics don't work well, because they can't penetrate the walled-off area. Surgery is usually necessary to expose the abscess and drain off the infection. Bring forth what is within you, and it will save you; do not bring it forth, and it will destroy you—in this case, literally.

In a similar vein, there are soldiers who have been wounded in battle by shrapnel. If this cannot be removed, the body simply closes up and tries to heal around it. Over time, however, a strange process can take place. The body begins to force the shrapnel to the surface. Years or even decades after the initial injury, bits of metal begin to poke through the skin. Again, there is a natural impulse to heal by bringing forth what's been hidden within. This is true for both the mind and the body. We must expose and expel what's been hidden in order to heal.

The secrets we fear to reveal behave much like shrapnel or abscesses. They are like foreign bodies strewn across the mind by emotional explosions from the past or infections that have festered into pockets of purulence. They poison the mind to the point where happiness becomes impossible and we hit bottom: we decide we've had enough and call them out for what they are—because we have no other choice. Yet in calling them out, we also discover what they are *not*. In God's reality, they are nothing. They do not exist, so, once brought forth, they melt away like ancient chunks of ice exposed to the hot summer sun.

The Course tells us we are dreaming. Our hidden shame and guilt about the separation are the foundation of that dream. As long as we remain asleep, this core shameful secret will haunt and frighten us. It will spin outward and take on many diverse forms, each giving rise to its own private nightmare. As we've seen, what occurs in a dream is unreal—but you cannot know that until you awaken.

You signal your willingness to awaken by bringing forth what is within you. Without the preservative of secrecy, your shame—shrapnel from the war of separation—begins to migrate toward the surface. Its power over you weakens. From within the dream, you begin to stir. You discover you are not reviled, because you did nothing wrong. You did not abandon God, nor did God abandon you. There is nothing to fear. Your long nightmare cracks open. Light streams in and begins the transformation to what the Course calls the "happy dream."

> *Children perceive frightening ghosts and monsters and dragons, and they are terrified. Yet if they ask someone they trust for the meaning of what they perceive, and are willing to let their own interpretations go in favor of reality, their fear goes with them. When a child is helped to translate his "ghost" into a curtain, his "monster" into a shadow, and his "dragon" into a dream he is no longer afraid, and laughs happily at his own fear.*[4]

> *If [children] ask for enlightenment and accept it, their fears vanish. But if they hide their nightmares they will keep*

them. . . . Little child, you are hiding your head under the cover of the heavy blankets you have laid upon yourself. You are hiding your nightmares in the darkness of your own false certainty, and refusing to open your eyes and look at them. Let us not save nightmares. . . . Take off the covers and look at what you are afraid of. Only the anticipation will frighten you, for the reality of nothingness cannot be frightening.[5]

*   *   *

Nathaniel Hawthorne's novel *The Scarlet Letter* paints a powerful portrait of the injunction to "bring forth" and the consequences of refusing to do so. The setting is Puritan New England in the seventeenth century. The protagonist, Hester Prynne, has sinned by giving birth to a child out of wedlock. The community is incensed. They want to know the identity of the father so he can be punished. But Hester refuses to reveal his name. She will not expose him. For her penance, she is forced to prominently display on her breast the letter A emblazoned in scarlet. The A marks her as an adulterer. She accepts this penance without shame. She does not protest or attempt to justify what she did. Nor does she try to run away in hopes of starting a new life elsewhere. She remains a member of the community and raises her illegitimate daughter, Pearl, in its midst in full view of everyone.

Throughout the novel, Hester carries herself with a sense of innate dignity. Her sin has been exposed for all to see, and so what? Life goes on. The scarlet letter A, intended to be a constant reminder of past sin, loses its power. Because it is exposed for all to see, it becomes old news. The past fades, overwritten by the present. We might say that Hester's perception of the letter A has shifted. It now stands for *acceptance*. And Hester's shift is mirrored outwardly as well by a shift in the attitude of the entire Puritan community. They come to accept her—scarlet letter, illegitimate child, and all.

By contrast, the child's father, Arthur Dimmesdale, remains hidden. He is the town's pastor, and to reveal what he has done would ruin him. But Hester's absent husband returns to the town and, sensing Dimmesdale's guilt, becomes his constant tormentor. Toward the end of the novel, we learn that Dimmesdale has his own scarlet letter. Unlike Hester's, which she carries in plain sight, Dimmesdale's A is hidden. It festers on his skin under his clothing, an open inflamed rash that none can see but himself. He has kept his secret concealed from everyone, and it eats away at him until at last he makes a public confession from the pulpit, openly embraces Hester and Pearl, and then dies. Hester brought forth what was within her, and it saved her. Dimmesdale could not bring forth what was within him (his sin, symbolized by his secret scarlet letter), and it destroyed him.

When it comes to understanding shame, its power over us and the path to freedom, *The Scarlet Letter* and the *Gospel of Thomas* get it right. Bringing forth what's hidden within is the path to healing. Recall that the introduction to the Course says that its aim is "*removing the blocks to the awareness of love's presence, which is your natural inheritance.*"[6] We don't need to manufacture love or bargain for it. It's always present: our natural inheritance from God. In truth, there *is* only love. Nothing else is real; nothing else exists. God is All. Therefore with God, nothing is hidden, because it can't be. There is no place to hide. How can anything pull away from what's all-encompassing to hide from its own identity? *"God hides nothing from His Son, even though His Son would hide himself. Yet the Son of God cannot hide his glory, for God wills him to be glorious, and gave him the light that shines in him."*[7]

We have not changed our essential nature, because that's simply not possible. This is the heart of the Course's message of freedom. It's not conditional. We don't have to *do* anything to achieve it. It's the nature of being, which is beyond anyone's power to change. As we've said before, the created cannot change their Creator or the nature of the Creator's creation. *"I am as God created me,"*[8] always and forever.

With this in mind, there is another way to understand the injunction to bring forth what is within you. Yes, guilt and shame live within you. They will continue to do so as long as you continue to believe in the ego's dream. It is imperative to bring forth that guilt and shame in order to heal yourself and awaken. But something else lives within you as well—beneath the guilt, beyond all shame—and it too must be brought forth in order to save you from dreaming. You already know what it is: your true Identity, the Self that God created sinless.

No matter how bad you think you've become, this true Self remains eternally loving, peaceful, and whole. You can refuse to recognize it. You can choose to look the other way and wander off into fields of illusion. Free will grants you that option, but it will not change your true nature.

This is the meaning of the parable of the Prodigal Son. No matter how far we think we stray, no matter how much we seem to squander our inheritance from God, we cannot lose it. The moment we choose to return home by remembering what we are, we are embraced.

Bore down past the shame and the layer upon layer of defenses employed to hide it; expose them for the illusions they are—and what do you find? What lies beneath? Love. Light. The Christ. The Ever-Mind. God's Son as God created him.

> *Do not be afraid to look within. The ego tells you all is black with guilt within you, and bids you not to look. . . . Within you is not what you believe is there, and what you put your faith in. Within you is the holy sign of perfect faith your Father has in you. . . . Look, then, upon the light He placed within you, and learn that what you feared was there has been replaced with love.*[9]

> *Think of your mind as a vast circle, surrounded by a layer of heavy, dark clouds. You can see only the clouds because you seem to be standing outside the circle and quite apart from it. From where you stand, you see no reason to believe there is a brilliant light hidden by the clouds. The clouds seem to be the only reality. They seem to be all there is to see. Therefore, you do not attempt to go through them and past them, which is the only way in which you would be really convinced of their lack of substance.*[10]

> *In shining peace within you is the perfect purity in which you were created. Fear not to look upon the lovely truth in you.*

Look through the cloud of guilt that dims your vision, and look past darkness to the holy place where you will see the light.[11]

Beyond the heavy, dark clouds of illusion lies the brilliant eternal light of the true Self. When the *Gospel of Thomas* preaches, "If you bring forth what is within you, then what is within you will save you," perhaps it is referring to this light as well. Bring forth the truth of your oneness with God, and that truth will be your salvation. Ignore it, overlook it, diminish its value in favor of any of the ego's goals—in other words, choose *not* to bring it forth—and that choice will destroy you. You will remain in darkness, ignorant of your true nature, scrabbling about in a world of pain and loss, disbelieving that you will ever see light and doubting that it even exists.

But we must qualify this statement in two ways. First, you cannot bring forth the light without piercing the clouds—and that requires the exposure and release of anything that blocks the light. Second, you cannot really destroy yourself, because, as we've said, you did not create yourself. The truth of what you are cannot *be* destroyed. That's the essence of the Atonement and its promise of salvation. You cannot change your identity except in dreams. The only thing that's ever vulnerable to destruction is your false self.

If you refuse to look within and bring forth the light in you, this false self will remain dominant—but only for a while, because it will never satisfy you, and it cannot fool you forever. When, after much pain, you finally understand this, you are presented once again with the possibility of renewal.

You always have the choice to change your mind and bring forth the light that lives eternally within you. In fact, the Course tells us that this "power of decision" is the *only* power remaining to you in your delusional dream state. It is "*your one remaining freedom as a prisoner of this world*."[12] So the real question becomes: How long before you make this choice? How much time will you fritter away enslaved to the ego? How much suffering are you willing to endure before you commit to awakening? "*In every difficulty, all distress, and each perplexity Christ calls to you and gently says, "My brother, choose again.*"[13] When you make that decision, time comes to an end, and you reenter Heaven.

*   *   *

We could debate which of these two interpretations of the passage from the *Gospel of Thomas* is more helpful. Some in the Course community focus primarily on the second meaning. Stay focused on the light, they will tell you. Bring it forth by doing your best to love everyone, no matter how you really feel about them, and it will shine away your ego. Others emphasize the first meaning and the need to expose the ego—its defenses, its futile goals, its false gods—and relentlessly strip them away one by one. They believe that only by recognizing these and dragging every last one of them to the truth can salvation be found.

But you need both of these perspectives, because they portray complementary truths. In theory, if we were able to make the decision once and for all to see our brothers, our sisters, and ourselves as sinless, imposing no judgments on them, we would bring forth only light: the holy Presence of the one true Self. But we can't—not yet and not consistently. We still have to work to free ourselves from guilt and shame. For now we need to make use of both interpretations. Both are necessary; neither is sufficient on its own.

We must never lose sight of the light within and the reality that we remain forever as God created us. But equally, we must not shy away from calling out the ego in its many guises in order to expose them and bring them forth into the light. Our sole task is to remove the blocks we have put up to the awareness of love's presence. To accomplish that, we should not overfocus on either interpretation at the expense of the other. We need both for healing. We must first bring forth the darkness that lives within us in order to bring forth the light.

Part Two
Grievance and Forgiveness

It is your forgiveness that will bring the darkness to the light. . . . Through your forgiveness does the truth about yourself return to your memory. Therefore, in your forgiveness lies your salvation.[1]

8

The Purpose of Relationship

Of all the spiritual teachings available today, *A Course in Miracles* may be unique in viewing relationships and not individual enlightenment as the path to awakening. The repurposing of special relationships to holy relationships is one of its central goals. Without this, it's not possible to return to your true Self.

The special relationships of the world are destructive, selfish and childishly egocentric. Yet, if given to the Holy Spirit, these relationships can become the holiest things on earth— the miracles that point the way to the return to Heaven. The world uses its special relationships as a final weapon of exclusion and a demonstration of separateness. The Holy Spirit transforms them into perfect lessons in forgiveness and in awakening from the dream. Each one is an opportunity to let perceptions be healed and errors corrected. Each one is another chance to forgive oneself by forgiving the other. And

*each one becomes still another invitation to the Holy Spirit
and to the remembrance of God.*[1]

According to the Course, salvation from the ego and
its illusions lies in relationships. They must be transformed
from tools of the ego to communication devices in service
of the Holy Spirit and God's plan of Atonement. The ego's
relationships are time-limited arrangements made and
transacted between separate individuals with differing life
stories and agendas; these may align or diverge at any given
time. In the Holy Spirit's hands, relationships become a
vehicle for the mutual recognition of holiness in minds
that are not separate but joined in oneness. By recognizing
holiness in others, we rekindle our own memory of it. In
this way, our relationships are transformed from special to
holy, and we reawaken to our true Identity as the Christ or
Ever-Mind.

Nevertheless, it's not *our* job to manufacture holiness
in our relationships. God has already done that by creat-
ing everyone holy. Our job is to expose and undo what we
taught ourselves about relationships and be willing to learn
from the Holy Spirit in order to see the holiness that God
created. *"The holy relationship . . . is learned. It is the old,
unholy relationship , transformed and seen anew."*[2] But we
will not see it unless we (1) *want* to see it, (2) actively search
out the *blocks* that keep us from seeing it, and (3) make
a *choice* to prioritize seeing it *over everything else.* As the
Course says in Workbook lessons 20 and 27, *"I am determined to see"* and *"Above all else I want to see."* In order to
see holiness and remember our true Self, we must part ways

with the ego and its craving for specialness—which cannot be shared—and embrace love and wholeness, which cannot *not* be shared. "*No gift of God can be unshared. It is this attribute that sets the gifts of God apart from every dream that ever seemed to take the place of truth.*"³ The goal of the relationship—and of relationships in general—must be changed to reflect this truth.

To the extent that you identify with the ego as a separate self, it will be impossible to see holiness in your relationships. Holiness, like truth, is shared. No one can be excluded from it. It has no exceptions, because even one small exception would pull you out of wholeness back into separation. Holiness must embrace all the seemingly separate bodies and selves you see everywhere around you in this world. "*Identity is shared,*"⁴ and relationship is the path that leads to the recognition of this sharing. "*I cannot come to You [God] without my brother. And to know my Source, I must first recognize what You created one with me. My brother's is the hand that leads me on the way to you.*"⁵

God cannot be approached by you as a separate individual, because you do not exist as an individual except within the dream. Sure, it's possible to reach some blissed-out states on your own, but you will not return to oneness alone because the concept of "alone" does not exist in God's reality. "*It is impossible to remember God in secret and alone. . . . The lonely journey fails, because it has excluded what it would find.*"⁶

If our true identity is shared, that is, if minds are joined in oneness, as they were in our original creation—if we are all nothing less than God's one Son, the Christ, the Ever-

Mind—how do we begin to recapture that oneness? How else but through relationship? *"It is only in relationships that salvation can be found."*[7] And *"A one-to-one relationship is not One Relationship. Yet it is the means of return: the way God chose for the return of His Son."*[8]

We use relationship to work our way back to wholeness when we make the commitment to see the other differently. The other is not an object to be manipulated or bargained with or to get something from. They are not an *it*, but a *thou*: a holy being in whom we behold the reflection of our own holiness. To achieve this, we proceed relationship by relationship, forgiving the grievances that cloud our vision of the other, no matter how small or insignificant they seem. The tiniest flicker of irritation will stand in the way of love and bar us from wholeness. In the same way, we must cleanse our relationships of all trace of specialness. Specialness depends on comparison—one particular thing, person, or outcome is judged as more desirable than another—and this too stands in the way of wholeness.

Through relationships, we discover the truth of who we are. They either reveal our shared identity and its holiness or they cloak it from our sight. Therefore, according to the Course, the fundamental unit of change on the journey to awakening is a relationship. *"The Holy Spirit's temple is not a body, but a relationship."*[9] That's where the real learning happens. That's our classroom, and the Holy Spirit is our tutor. *"Under His teaching, every relationship becomes a lesson in love."*[10]

Every relationship offers us another opportunity to choose between holiness and specialness, Christ or the ego,

Ever-Mind or Never-Mind—every day and every minute of the day. According to the Course, this is the purpose of all relationships. It is their only real purpose.

Relationship: The Real Thing

If we rigorously apply the Course's teaching to our own lives, it becomes apparent that *all* of our relationships must change: not just the ones that we select out and designate as special—friends, lovers, rivals—but all the other boring, vanilla, unspecial ones as well. Why? Because in our separated state, we are incapable of distinguishing between what's special and holy. We're too identified with the ego.

If we're perfectly honest, we'll acknowledge that *all of our relationships are special* in one form or another. We judge each in terms of its good and bad qualities. What does the other person offer us? Do they agree with our opinions, laugh at our jokes, provide us with material things we lack? If so, that's "good" special. Do they make us feel sad, scared, ashamed, or angry? That's special too: "bad" special. We enjoy those who support our self-image by seeing us as we want to be seen; we dislike those who challenge and undermine that image. In this way, the ego uses relationships not to communicate, not to join together, but to reinforce its own separate identity.

The Holy Spirit uses relationships for the opposite purpose: to free us from the ego's grip and restore our true identity. Each relationship entrusted to His care undergoes a change in purpose. It no longer serves our needs as we saw them from the ego's perspective, as separate individuals. It now serves the goal of uniting us at the level of spirit. Each relationship becomes a stepping-stone along the pathway to oneness and the Self we all share.

The Holy Spirit does not recognize preference or hierarchy in relationships. None is more valuable than any other, or less valuable. To Him, they are all of equal importance and equally deserving of love. Each relationship has exactly the same purpose: forgiveness. Each must be healed.

> *There is no order in relationships. They either are or not. An unholy relationship is no relationship. It is a state of isolation, which seems to be what it is not. No more than that. The instant that the mad idea of making your relationship with God unholy seemed to be possible, all your relationships were made meaningless.*[11]

In other words, what we consider to be a relationship between two separate individuals is really just a cover-up intended to mask the underlying isolation of the ego. It's a big nothing. Yet this is the only relationship the solitary ego understands. The holy relationship lies forever beyond its reach. This is not some cruel jest or punishment from God. It's simply a restatement of the ego's essential nature. It *is* alone, by definition, and "*God cannot be remembered alone.*"[12] The Course also says, "*The Kingdom [of God] cannot be found alone, and you who are the Kingdom cannot find yourself alone. To achieve the goal of the curriculum, then, you cannot listen to the ego.*"[13]

As we saw in *From Never-Mind to Ever-Mind*, the ego is an unreliable guide on the road to awakening. It will use relationships and everything else in your life as a diversion: a way to preserve itself and hurt you. Your only real relationship is with God as His one Son, the perfect extension of His Love.

The Christ—the Ever-Mind—still lives in each of us, even if we blind ourselves to it. That you cannot change. You cannot change what God created you to be. It is the only reality. When you remember this Self, you will be happy, because that is what you were created to be. There is no real alternative.

Unfortunately, this insight, however powerful, is often not helpful to us in our current separated state, identified as we are with the ego. How then do we set about repairing the breach with God and with our true Self, a breach that exists in our mind, but not in God's? How do we heal the fractured Sonship? Relationship by relationship.

9

Repairing the Shattered Son of God

We have lost our way and wandered into a world of shifting dreams under the dominion of the ego. But as we've seen, we cannot shut out truth completely, because it is part of us. "*The laws of love are not suspended because you sleep.*"[1] Truth constantly pushes up against the boundaries of the illusion, poking to find a chink in our defenses in order to slip through and coax us toward awakening. It does this gently, patiently, but urgently—like a parent at the bedside of a comatose child, whispering words of love and support, holding and squeezing the child's hand, trusting that at some deep level their words and love are getting through and will help awaken the child from her unconscious state. Such a parent would do anything to bring their child out of her coma. Would God be any less determined to awaken His sleeping Son?

Therefore no single religion or spiritual system can lay claim to truth as its exclusive property. (If it does, you can be sure that it serves the ego and not God.) Truth cannot be confined or limited to a single set of beliefs. It will filter through in all languages and cultures, in every era and epoch, in countless forms, and to anyone who is ready to hear it. Like a calm, relentless tide, it laps against the bulwarks we erected to keep it out, and eventually it will breach them all. It never lets up, because it is eternal. Our defenses cannot prevail against it. They can only postpone the final reckoning, or rather the reconciliation in which all illusion vanishes in the light of truth.

"No one . . . is able to deny truth totally, even if he thinks he can."[2] Give truth the slightest opening, and it will shine through. As a result, certain ideas found in the Course turn up in other spiritual systems and religions as well. How could it be otherwise?

Tikkun Olam: Repair of the World

Mystical Judaism contains a teaching that attempts to explain how the world of separation came into being. It goes by the name *tikkun olam* (restoration of the world). According to this idea, in order to create the world, God poured the essence of His Being into a vessel of light. But somehow the vessel fell and shattered, fragmenting God's creation into countless bits and pieces of light, all now separate and scattered about, bound within a world of physical matter. Those broken fragments of God's creation are *us*: the billions of residents of planet earth. It is the sacred duty of each person to help repair the fracture and reunite these scattered pieces of creation back into the oneness that God originally intended for them. *Tikkun olam* is the Jewish equivalent of the Course's Atonement. We can see this even from the terminology used in these Course quotes:

It should especially be noted that God has only one Son. If all His creations are His Sons, every one must be an integral part of the whole Sonship. The Sonship in its oneness transcends the sum of its parts. However, this is obscured as long as any of its parts is missing. That is why the conflict cannot ultimately be resolved until all the parts of the Sonship have returned. The correction of this error is the Atonement.[3]

You who believe that God is fear made but one substitution . . . the substitution of illusion for truth; of fragmentation for wholeness. It has become so splintered and subdivided and divided again, over and over, that it is now almost impossible to perceive it once was one, and still is what it was. That one error . . . was all you ever made. . . . But nothing you have seen begins to show you the enormity of the original error, which seemed to cast you out of Heaven, to shatter knowledge into meaningless bits of disunited perceptions, and to force you to make further substitutions.[4]

What is the world except a little gap perceived to tear eternity apart, and break it into days and months and years? And what are you who live within the world except a picture of the Son of God in broken pieces, each concealed within a separate and uncertain bit of clay?[5]

In the traditional Jewish interpretation of *tikkun olam*, we repair the shattered fragments of God's creation by performing good deeds for our fellow humans. According to the Course, however, such a plan cannot succeed. Why not? Because good deeds take place within the ego's dream world. They are performed by those who still believe that they are separate from each other and who therefore lack the ability to judge what is truly helpful.

Any particular good deed that we choose to perform may or may not prove helpful in advancing the Atonement. This is because those performing these deeds don't see the big picture. However well-intended, their deeds can and often do misfire, especially when hijacked by the ego for its own purposes. Think of it as the law of unintended consequences. You give money to a good cause and learn it was squandered. You save a child from drowning, and he grows up to be a murderer. Because we are lost in illusion, we cannot see how our actions, our money, or our caring might best be applied. For that we need the Holy Spirit's overview and guidance.

*   *   *

The Course tells us that we "*need do nothing*"[6] to bring about the holy instant, in which illusions end. *Doing* requires a body; minds do not *do* anything. Actions taken from within a dream will not end dreaming. For this reason, the Course does not advocate performing good deeds as a means of saving the world. "*Therefore, seek not to change the world, but choose to change your mind about the world. Perception is a result and not a cause.*"[7] If we want to change the world—to do the work of *tikkun olam* and repair the separation from God and each other—we must open our minds to the Holy Spirit and become miracle workers.

A miracle is not a deed. Although it takes place at the level of the dream world and the separated self, it originates at the level of the mind, which we share. Therefore it addresses the cause, not the effect: the dreamer, not the dream. It may or may not have observable effects within the dream, but that's beside the point, because we are not in any position to judge. Lacking the big picture, we see things only in fragments or, as the Bible puts it, "through a glass darkly." That's just the nature of perception. (This is discussed at length in chapter 2 of *From Never-Mind to Ever-Mind*.)

Miracles save time as we understand it. A grievance or conflict that might have taken a lifetime to work itself out can resolve in the space of an instant. As we learn to do the work of forgiveness and accept God's plan of Atonement, we become miracle workers. Our own change of mind about what we are and why we're here is all that's needed. We make the decision to forgive, to shift from a fearful vision to a loving one; the Holy Spirit does the rest, reaching out to other minds through ours.

> *Miracles are part of an interlocking chain of forgiveness which, when completed, is the Atonement. Atonement works all the time and in all dimensions of time.*[8]

> *The forgiven are the means of the Atonement. Being filled with spirit, they forgive in return. Those who are released must join in releasing their brothers, for this is the plan of the Atonement. Miracles are the way in which minds that serve the Holy Spirit unite with me [Jesus] for the salvation or release of all of God's creations.*[9]

Now we can begin to appreciate the essential role played by relationships in the Atonement and *tikkun olam*. Relationships are not limited, one-on-one arrangements—not unless we see ourselves as egos and bodies. They are stepping-stones to Spirit. Each relationship invites us to make a decision, a profound decision, and the only one with real meaning. Do we choose to see others as individual beings with separate interests and agendas that differ from our own? If so, we will judge them, attacking and defending. Or do we let the Holy Spirit show us another way of seeing? He can teach us to look past differences in order to behold the light of oneness within each of us, a light that does not change or vary in its brilliance. This is the same light we experience in "the perfect moment" (described in chapter 3 of *From Never-Mind to Ever-Mind*). It has nothing to do with the physical eye. It is a luminosity that infuses all we see. In its radiance the sight of bodies and differences fades away. In their place we rediscover the oneness of our true Self.

A Dissociative Model of Separation

In the second-to-last chapter of *From Never-Mind to Ever-Mind* I discussed in some detail the nature of dissociation as a psychological defense mechanism and how it manifests in the extreme in the psychiatric disorder known officially as *dissociative identity disorder* (DID) and informally as *multiple personality*. The Course tells us that separation and dissociation are synonymous and that "*the separation was and is dissociation*."[10] DID may offer the best model for understanding our predicament as shattered pieces of God's creation and how to fix it.

DID results from trauma so severe that it overwhelms the mind, which splits into any number of what appear to be different personalities. Each of these "alter personalities" believes that it is separate and distinct from all the others. Each lives in its own captivatingly real inner world. These worlds are often nightmarish, filled with echoes of abuse, but nonetheless, to the alters they are reality. Alter personalities may or may not be aware of one another. They frequently have conflicting agendas. More often than not they dislike and distrust one another.

To an observer, it is obvious that alters share the same body. Nonetheless, they reject this idea and will actively resist any information that supports it because it is so threatening to their individual senses of self. Only when they gain the experience of greater peace and happiness through treatment do they begin to relax their grip on the need to remain separate and open up to the possibility of working together and ultimately merging with one another.

We are very much like these alter personalities. Why would we give up our precious individuality and the relationships that support it for some crazy notion of wholeness? The Course's worldview must seem insane, and threatening, until we experience its effects. Only when we feel more at peace, when our relationships become more loving, when we witness miracles of forgiveness, will we be willing to consider the possibility that all we thought we knew about ourselves and the world might be wrong.

Experience alone can convince us. Without validation in experience, we cannot simply accept the idea that minds are joined and that our true identity is far grander than anything we could imagine. That is what the practice of *A Course in Miracles* brings to us.

To those convinced that their delusions are real, truth must appear insane. They will defend their delusions against its encroachment even to the point of death. Illusions are not given up lightly. To the extent we invest belief in them, they will mirror back to us their seeming reality. Like many other metaphysical systems, the Course tells us that belief determines perception: we will quite literally see what we want to see and what we need to believe is real.

> *When you believe something, you have made it true for you.*[11]
>
> *What you desire, you will see. And if its reality is false, you will uphold it by not realizing all the adjustments you have introduced to make it so.*[12]

For example, if you believe that someone is guilty of a crime, you will view them through the lens of your belief and see them as guilty. They will appear to be sneaking around, engaging in suspicious activity. Perhaps you follow them to report on their activity to the police, and they discover this and start to run (because they're afraid of *you*). Your behavior toward them has provoked a response that confirms your original belief. Perception—what we think we see and hear—is an effect, not a cause. Misperceptions can only be corrected at their source, which is the mind.

Giving Relationships to the Holy Spirit

We, the deluded, sleepwalk through our private dreams of separation and death. We invest them with belief, which keeps them real *for us.* Our relationships reflect those beliefs back to us and in the process make them stronger. But what we believe about our fellow humans is not their reality. To have any chance of experiencing that, we need the Holy Spirit. In one relationship after another, we release our interpretation of the other person and their behavior to the Holy Spirit. He reinterprets them for us, viewing them through the lens of truth, seeing them as God would see them. In that view, their only purpose is forgiveness. Whether it is a love triangle, a business partnership, a demented parent, or a rebellious child, the Holy Spirit sees no differences. They're part of *our* dream, and His function is to awaken us from that dream, not join us in it. We borrow His vision to learn the meaning of love, and it is inseparable from oneness.

We are love and nothing but love, created by love, eternally love—all of us, without exception. In Christ's vision, the vision of the Ever-Mind, there can be no differences between us. Anything we perceive that is *not* love is just another barrier that we put up to block God from our awareness. If we want love and the joy it brings, we have to tear down those barriers. The main stumbling block to this—the only one, in fact—is our willingness. We must be willing to remove the blinders from our eyes and let the Holy Spirit show us this new way of seeing. "*When you want only love you will see only love.*"[13]

Here then is true intimacy: *into-me-see.* We see into everyone, but what we see has nothing to do with flaws or character defects. It has nothing to do with bodies, personalities, or behavior. We look past these. They are mere shadows that vanish in the blaze of light of the true Self. We see holiness, and we cannot help but love what we see, because it lives in us too. And so we welcome everyone to behold that same light shining from within us. Again, we want to bring forth that holy light and together bear witness to its shared reality. "*Holiness must be shared, for therein lies everything that makes it holy.*"[14] In light, we are joined with everyone.

We can only share what is real; the rest is nothingness, and we simply let it go. It has no more meaning for us. The need for hiding is gone too, because the things we wanted to keep hidden only block the light. Why would we want that now?

The ego will protest. It will tell you that to share holiness is to lose all chance at specialness. Why take that risk? Why give up all you've ever known and wanted? But the Holy Spirit will not make your special relationships disappear in a blaze of light. To use the metaphor of DID, he does not dissolve the alter personalities you thought to be real. Rather he works through you to transform the very idea of relationship: from limited fantasies of special love to the reality of all-inclusive, holy Love.

That is what the Holy Spirit does in the special relationship. He does not destroy it, nor snatch it away from you. But He does use it differently, as a help to make His purpose real to you. The special relationship will remain, not as a source of pain and guilt, but as a source of joy and freedom. It will not be for you alone, for therein lay its misery. As its unholiness kept it a thing apart, its holiness will become an offering to everyone.

Your special relationship will be a happy dream, and one which you will share with all who come within your sight.[15]

We give the Holy Spirit our private individual mind, and in return He gives us the one mind of the Sonship. We trade illusion for the real world. That's a very good deal. It's better than any bargain the ego could strike.

In this world, God's Son comes closest to himself in a holy relationship. There he begins to find the certainty his Father has in him. And there he finds his function of restoring his Father's laws to what was held outside them, and finding what was lost. Only in time can anything be lost, and never lost forever. So do the parts of God's Son gradually join in time, and with each joining is the end of time brought nearer. Each miracle of joining is a mighty herald of eternity. No one who has a single purpose, unified and sure, can be afraid. No one who shares his purpose with him can not be one with him.[16]

As specialness gives way to holiness, the fragments of the shattered Son of God reunite, pieced together by the loving hands of the Holy Spirit, fulfilling the true goal of *tikkun olam*. Relationship has now served its true purpose and become a vehicle for healing: the path back to wholeness. Special relationships have transformed into holy relationships. Eventually, relationship itself—even holy relationship—dissolves back into the seamless Oneness that is God and God's Son.

10

Holding Grievances

My maternal grandmother, Minnie, was a good person. She loved her family more than she loved herself and would have done anything for her grandchildren. And yet she could sure hold a grievance.

When my parents divorced in the late 1960s, Minnie blamed my father. Of course, he bore a lot of the responsibility for the split. But as a seasoned couples therapist, I can say that, with rare exceptions, every divorce has at least two sides. Like the characters in the classic Kurosawa film *Rashomon*, each person involved in the drama, as well as those who only witness it from outside, will have their own account of what happened. But Minnie wasn't interested in my father's account or in any version that allowed him to escape full blame. He had hurt her daughter—period. Nothing else mattered.

To make her point, Minnie took scissors to her collection of family photographs and cut out my father's image from each one. This resulted in some rather awkward-looking portraits, but rather than finding that embarrassing, it was as if Minnie wanted to put them on display for everyone to see—as if they were the visual representation of what my father had done to her heart and her family. As a courtesy, we grandchildren never talked about our father in her presence.

In a short time, both my parents remarried. Their new spouses proved to be far better matches temperamentally. Everyone got along; no one slandered anyone else. When my parents welcomed their own new grandchildren into the family, any remaining barriers dissolved. Without much discussion and with no reservations, we began celebrating birthdays and holidays together again as a family. My dad and stepmom would invite everyone to their house on one occasion, and my mom and stepdad would do the same on another. The events were loud and boisterous, but not from rancor—just a typical Jewish family talking over each other in total agreement. Sadly absent from these gatherings were my grandparents. (My grandfather remained close to my father, secretly paying visits to him at his office. But Minnie could never know.)

Minnie took her grievance against my father with her to the grave. It had been forged in the heat of a painful divorce, but she kept the fires stoked and burning in her mind long after they'd cooled to ashes for everyone else. As with her family photos, she'd taken a narrow slice of the past during which a divorce had occurred, enlarged it by excising any contravening information, laminated it with recrimination, and turned it into something unforgivable.

To what end? Revenge? Did it hurt my father? At first, perhaps. But once the families had come together again, he was happy. The only person still hurting was Minnie. She'd kept the past alive at the expense of the present and deprived herself of the joy of a family reunited. Of course she never knew what she was missing, because she was never willing to give forgiveness a chance and join the rest of us. She'd tried to expel my father from the family, but in reality the one she expelled was herself.

A Buddhist teaching aptly portrays this double-edged aspect of grievances. It goes something like this: holding a grievance is like thrusting a sword through your mid-section in order to the wound the offender who's standing behind you. You may succeed, but the consequences will prove more deadly for you than for them.

Another good analogy is that a grievance is like a hot coal that you hurl at the person who wronged you. In order to throw it, you must first grasp it in your own hand. Whether you hit them or miss wildly, either way you'll be burned. Better by far to leave the hot coal where it lies and pick up an olive branch instead.

"All that I do I do unto myself. If I attack, I suffer. But if I forgive, salvation will be given me."[1] Grievances truly are double-edged swords, and the edge facing you turns out to be the sharpest.

Grievance as Attack

Unless you're born a saint, it is impossible to go through life without at some point holding grievances. These could be about almost anything: the jar with the tight lid that refuses to open, the traffic light that turns red just as you approach, the sports team that humiliates the hometown favorite in the playoffs, traffic backed up on the freeway, the appliance that breaks down at the worst possible moment. But the grievances that stick with us most are focused on other people. This is inevitable, given the nature of the ego and its idea of relationship. No two people see things exactly the same way. Therefore conflict becomes unavoidable. It is intrinsic to all human relationships.

Grievances come in all shapes and sizes, ranging from mild pique to a murderous craving for revenge. But grievances do not emerge from nowhere. As with Minnie, they are our response to a perceived hurt or insult. Someone or something has wounded us and we have judged that wound to be so painful, so difficult to heal, that we refuse even to consider the possibility. We prefer instead to hold on to it, to poke at it regularly, turning it over in our minds, reliving the event that hurt us so much. We wear it like a badge—a constant reminder of the injustice we suffered.

*   *   *

To hold a grievance is to launch an attack and, as we have seen, we attack when we feel less than or at-lack. Hurts and insults fuel a sense of inferiority. Someone has dared to challenge the self-image we tried to sell to the world. We can't just let that slide; we have to retaliate somehow.

We overcome the bite of shame by launching a counter-attack against its source, whatever we perceive that source to be. In this sense, grievances are very much an example of the attack-other defense against shame. The grievance serves as a kind of covert mental assault, a way of striking back at the person we believe has shamed us.

My grandmother Minnie was ashamed of her daughter's divorce. She managed that shame through attack-other by leveling a grievance against my father. I don't know the strength of my grandparents' marriage. I do know that they were very different personalities, and as a result there was conflict. But as immigrants to the United States, they were tied to each other through good times and bad. The thought of divorce would never have occurred to them. My grandmother saw my parents' separation as a blow to her fundamental belief that spouses stick together no matter what. To the extent that she had sacrificed to stay in her less than satisfying marriage, she expected her son-in-law to do the same. But he failed those expectations. The divorce challenged her belief in sacrifice and called into question how she'd chosen to live her life. My father wasn't playing by the same set of rules, and she found it impossible to let that slide. He must be punished, if only to counter her own fear that her beliefs about marriage might be wrong and her sacrifice for naught. *That* would be even more shameful!

Shame and grievance walk hand in hand. Where one goes, the other cannot be far behind.

Strangely, one of the most common targets for grievances is God. When bad things happen, like mass shootings, natural disasters, or cancer in children, we ask how God could have allowed it. What did we or they do to deserve this? We feel like victims, persecuted unfairly, like Job in the Bible, manipulated by forces greater than ourselves. This harks back to childhood, when we had very little control over what happened to us. It is also an accurate picture of the ego's world, because its sense of control is pure fiction. At any moment, everything could fall cataclysmically apart. And of course feeling you have no control is a source of profound fear and shame.

To hold a grievance against God reflects a fundamental misunderstanding of His nature. It casts Him in the role of an all-knowing, all-powerful force that lives outside of us and looks down in judgment to find us lacking. If we believe that God is the source of our injury and the shame it provokes—and how could it be otherwise if He truly is all-knowing and powerful?—we will assail Him with grievances.

Rather than looking inward for the source of guilt and shame, we make God into something He could never be and offload our blame onto Him. It's yet another example of the ego's bait-and-switch tactics. Take the worst traits of ego—arrogance and judgment—project them onto the ego's fearful image of God, and then react to that image by holding a grievance against it. Essentially we've deployed the attack-other defense against God. Yet if God is the only way out of the ego's prison (through His representative, the Holy Spirit), then blaming Him is certain to keep us there. Which of course is what the ego wants.

The Ego's Plan for Salvation

The ego's concept of self is shaky. The self-image it tries to sell you is a ruse designed to cover up its core insecurity. The Course tells us that *"the ego's fundamental wish is to replace God,"*[2] yet it knows full well this could never happen. Its quest to replace God is a narcissistic fantasy doomed to fail, no matter how it tries to spin it. The ego also knows that while *it* is nothing, *you* are God's creation, as much like Him as He is to Himself. This drives the ego mad, and it retaliates with grievances: against God, against you, against your fellow humans—against pretty much anything, as long as it keeps you focused away from truth.

> *You may not realize that the ego has set up a plan for salvation in opposition to God's. It is this plan in which you believe. . . . The ego's plan for salvation centers around holding grievances. It maintains that, if someone else spoke or acted differently, if some external circumstance or event were changed, you would be saved. Thus, the source of salvation is constantly perceived as outside yourself. Each grievance that you hold is a declaration, an assertion in which you believe, that says, "If this were different, I would be saved." The change of mind necessary for salvation is thus demanded of everyone and everything except yourself.* [3]

Grievances are investments in illusion. If the outer world is merely a projection of the mind, seeking outside yourself must fail, because healing can only be found from within. As we noted, it is impossible to achieve meaningful change without addressing the *source* of the problem instead of its *effects*. And the source is the delusional mind that dreamed itself into being as the ego.

In part 1, we saw that it is essential to bring forth the darkness within us so that we can bring forth the light. Now we go further. It is not enough to expose and release your own shame. That's only part of the solution. To be free, it is also necessary to forgive your grievances against others. Grievances will block you from love and your true Self as surely as the deepest personal shame. They will infect every relationship you have. You cannot be free while seeking to keep others imprisoned.

The Course reminds us that a jailer is as much a prisoner as the one he guards. The lives of both depend upon those prison bars; they simply view them from opposite sides. Neither is free to get up and leave—not unless they give up their assigned roles. To be free, the jailer must let go of all desire to imprison, while the prisoner must learn to value the jailer as her only sure road to freedom. The grievances they lodge against each other will keep them both bound together and stuck behind bars.

You who were created by love like itself can hold no griev-ances and know your Self. To hold a grievance is to forget who you are. To hold a grievance is to see yourself as a body. To hold a grievance is to let the ego rule your mind and condemn the body to death. Perhaps you do not yet fully realize just what holding grievances does to your mind. It seems to split you off from your Source and make you unlike Him. . . .

Shut off from your Self, which remains aware of Its like-ness to Its Creator, your Self seems to sleep, while the part of your mind that weaves illusions in its sleep appears to be

awake. Can all this arise from holding grievances? Oh, yes!
For he who holds grievances denies he was created by love,
and his Creator has become fearful to him in his dream of
hate. Who can dream of hatred and not fear God? [4]

Here is the true cost of holding grievances. They cast aside the goal of *tikkun olam*. They keep us from repairing our one true Self and experiencing its peace. Given this, why would anyone choose to hold a grievance? We must commit to letting go of grievances. We must learn to forgive.

11

Releasing the Past

Grievances never occur in the present tense. They are never about what's happening *now*, in this moment. They are ghosts from the past that feed off memory to haunt the present.

Grievances are remembered, not experienced. But they reach out from their perch in memory to ensnare us, binding us to people and events long gone.

A grievance is a way of keeping the past alive. As we saw with Minnie, it is a choice to honor what hurt us and prioritize it over present happiness. It's like acid, eating away at our peace of mind, eroding any hope of satisfaction in the present. *How can I feel good when that horrible person did that mean thing to me?* We find ourselves fantasizing about revenge or the clever things we should have said to handle the situation better. But these do not help us. Rather they fuel the grievance and give it greater strength.

When Past Denies Present

Hiroo Onoda was a loyal Japanese soldier with a proud samurai ancestry. Trained in guerilla warfare and counter-intelligence, he was posted to a small island in the Philippines during the final months of World War II. When the Japanese forces on the island were defeated in February 1945, he and three other soldiers retreated into the jungle to wage a guerilla campaign, exactly as he'd been ordered to do. He was a good soldier.

In August of that year, following the destruction of Hiroshima and Nagasaki, the emperor of Japan surrendered. Onoda never got the news. He and his small band continued to raid local villages, stealing food and wreaking havoc, then dissolving back into the jungle.

In an attempt to reach stray elements of the Japanese army like Onoda's group, leaflets proclaiming the end of the war were air-dropped over many islands in the Philippines. Onoda saw these but dismissed them as propaganda. He did not believe the imperial Japanese army would ever surrender.

One of his band came to realize the leaflets were genuine and gave himself up to local authorities. He revealed the identities of the holdouts, making it possible to airdrop family photos and personal pleas for Onoda and his companions to return home. Onoda assumed that his family had been coerced into providing these photos by an American occupation force.

This situation persisted for twenty-nine years. Finally in 1974 a Japanese adventurer and admirer of Onoda's tracked him down in the jungle and learned from him that only a direct command from his superior officer would cause him to lay down his arms. That officer, now a civilian, was located, flown to the Philippines, and taken to Onoda to issue the final order to surrender. And so at last the war came to an end for Hiroo Onoda.

Many in Japan greeted Onoda as a hero, an exemplar of duty and loyalty to country. But he also serves as an example of how a grievance—in this case, a national grievance forged in wartime—can be perpetuated to the point of absurdity. Lives were lost and years wasted as a result of his actions.

Onoda obviously prioritized the past in the form of his commanding officer's orders over the present. He rejected new information that could have allowed him to release the past, like the photos and letters from his family, interpreting them instead in a manner that supported his beliefs about the war and his country. Was he a hero for such behavior? Or was he a deluded fool whose obstinacy cost him almost thirty years of his life, years that could have been spent in peace with his family?

Onoda beautifully demonstrates what the Course tells us about an unforgiving thought and our resistance to forgiveness.

An unforgiving thought is one which makes a judgment that it will not raise to doubt, although it is not true. The mind is closed, and will not be released. . . .

An unforgiving thought does many things. In frantic action it pursues its goal, twisting and overturning what

it sees as interfering with its chosen path. Distortion is its
purpose, and the means by which it would accomplish it
as well. It sets about its furious attempts to smash reality,
without concern for anything that would appear to pose a
contradiction to its point of view.[1]

To maintain a grievance—an unforgiving thought—
requires work. Truth will reach out to correct it in many
ways through many different people. Its approaches must
be rejected, as they were by Onoda. Grievances enshrine
the past as the only thing that matters. They keep you
chained to old beliefs formed in response to a different time
and a different you. They overrule the present.

If we want to diminish the power that the past holds
over us, we need to give it a different meaning. We need to
recognize and accept the signs that the war is over—that
there is no further justification for grievances and that there
never really was, except in our own minds. We need to allow
that new information to sink in and shift our interpretation
of the past and the grievance it gave birth to. This can come
in the form of a therapeutic reframe, as we saw in chapter
6 (including of course the Holy Spirit's ultimate reframe),
or we can address it even more broadly. We can learn that
memory itself is nothing more than a subjective reconstruc-
tion of the past. It can never be trusted as accurate.

As was discussed in *From Never-Mind to Ever-Mind*, the
information brought to us through the organs of the five
senses is limited. We are not all-seeing and all-knowing.
Our eyes and ears can and do fail us in many ways. Thus the
memories formed by our perceptions can be faulty as well.

Furthermore, it's not events themselves that lead us to form grievances; it's our *interpretation* of those events. If we can accept that our interpretations are inherently flawed, shaped by beliefs that run so deep they're seldom recognized, we can more easily dismiss them as fabrications and free ourselves from the burden of the past. After all, if we know that the memory behind a grievance is unreliable, we should be more willing to let the grievance go.

Memory: It Ain't What It Used to Be

As anyone past the age of fifty can testify, it is very easy to forget. But psychology tells us that it is also possible to "remember" things that never happened. If we've heard the details of some event witnessed by other people, people we trust—especially if we've heard these details repeated many times—we naturally construct visual images to go along with what we've heard, and these can give rise to a false memory. This sometimes occurs in younger siblings, who have been told stories about things they did when they were a baby, which they later claim to remember. Similarly, we can incorporate elements of someone else's life or even scenes from a novel or movie as if they were our own. We can also make things up outright. If we recite the imagined details often enough, eventually they become real to us. They become "memories."

In my last year of high school, some friends and I rented a beach house in Wildwood, New Jersey, over the Memorial Day weekend. It was a full-on party scene for graduating seniors. One night I had a few more beers than was advisable (the drinking age was eighteen back then), and while navigating a busy street I sideswiped a parked car. I didn't stop, but later I discovered that it left a good-sized dent along the passenger-side door of my car. I did not want to confess my misdeed to my parents, so I made up a story. I told them how crazy the town was that weekend, with inebriated kids crowding all the bars and how I emerged from a bar and went to my car (parked of course on the left side of a one-way street) and found this horrific dent. Some drunken teen must have sideswiped the car. I was basically an honest kid, so my parents never questioned my account. And it wasn't all that far from the truth!

I imagined this scene very vividly in my mind: walking up to the car, seeing the dent, and reacting with disbelief and anger. My mental imagery was reinforced in later years, when I did in fact have that exact experience of approaching my car and discovering damage caused by some random driver. The result was a fabricated memory. For years, whenever the town of Wildwood, New Jersey, came up in conversation, I'd shake my head in disapproval and repeat the story of how some drunk kid had sideswiped my car. The memory became quite real for me. Then one day, as I was telling the story for the umpteenth time, I remembered that it was not true. Yet that did not eradicate the false memory I'd constructed for myself. Instead I was left with two parallel "memories" of the same incident: one that happened and one that I wanted to have happened. Even today the false memory is more vivid and feels more real.

It is also possible to fabricate memories when two closely related events become conjoined into a single memory. Psychiatrist Lenore Terr, in her book *Too Scared to Cry*, describes a case in which a ten year-old Eastern European immigrant was scolded and shamed by an angry Asian shop owner.[2] The young girl then ran outside to cross the street and was hit by a car. When telling her story two years later, she swore that the driver of the car that hit her was Asian, just like the shop owner. She was absolutely certain of this—she'd seen his face before she was struck—even though the police report clearly documented that the driver was white. It didn't matter. Two powerful traumatic memories occurring closely together had fused into one in her mind. This girl knew what she "saw" and had a very hard time believing otherwise.

Stories like these demonstrate that memory is often fallible and cannot be trusted implicitly. It rests on assumptions and incomplete judgments, which then generate more of the same. We must remain open to questioning what we remember and to modifying it in light of new evidence, especially if the memory has hardened into a grievance.

The Anatomy of Grievances

I said earlier that relationships are the classrooms in which the Holy Spirit teaches us how to remember that we are spirit and identical to each other in holiness. Grievances stand in the way of this recognition. The Holy Spirit will not be able to help us unless we're willing to look honestly at those grievances and forgive them.

If it is our interpretation of events that leads to grievance formation, and if we can accept that those interpretations are not necessarily factual, it should become easier to question them. Minnie believed her daughter had been hurt and shamed by the divorce, because that's how *she* would have felt. It was *her* interpretation, not my mother's. Had she been able to hear my mother's perspective or witness the healing that occurred in the family over time, she could have let her interpretation go, along with the grievance.

To demonstrate the power of interpretations, let's consider three different scenarios, each with the potential to generate a grievance. You may not have encountered these exact sets of circumstances, but you've probably come close enough that they won't seem unfamiliar.

1. You enter an elevator. Two adolescent boys huddle in the corner whispering to each other. As the doors slide shut and you hit the button for your floor, one of them glances in your direction, breaks into a grin, murmurs something to the other, and they both begin to snicker with laughter. You're pretty sure they're laughing at you, but you have no idea why.

2. You've been working at your job for a couple of years, and you've made two good friends. You've collaborated with them on projects, hung out at parties, cooked together, laughed together, dished dirt on your bosses, and shared your philosophies about life, love, and success. One day you learn that your two good friends went to a concert without you. They didn't ask if you wanted to join them; they made no mention of their plans. You were excluded for no reason that you know of.

3. Your older brother has cut off all communication with you. You've known and looked up to him your entire life. You've shared holidays, family celebrations, and hardships of all kinds. But now he won't return your texts, calls, or emails. You beg him for some explanation, but get no reply. You know he's alive and well; you've seen the photos he posts on Facebook. He simply no longer seems to want you in his life, and you have no idea why. You're baffled and deeply hurt, and grow increasingly angry every time you think about him.

Regarding all three examples, ask yourself the following questions:

1. How would this make you feel if it were you?
2. What would you do about it, and why?
3. What outcome would you hope for?
4. Assuming you can't get explanations and can't change things, how long would this situation continue to bother you? Would it become a grievance?
5. Are you more likely to blame yourself or the other? That is, would you feel guilty over something you think *you* must have done, even if you can't figure out what that was? Or would you see yourself as the one who was wronged and therefore fully justified in your reactions, whatever they may be?

Your answers to these questions will depend largely on how you interpret each situation. This in turn will depend on your past experience.

Let's start with the teens in the elevator. If you happen to be the parent of teenage boys and are familiar with their antics, you might dismiss the whole incident as no big deal; it's just how teenage boys behave. You excuse it and exit the elevator with a smile, never bothering to think about it again. But if you have a teenage daughter who came home from school in tears the other day because she was teased by some boys in her class, you might feel differently. Your daughter's experience would color your reaction. You might say something to them or decide to go frosty and ignore them with malice. If you continue to hold this incident in your mind, keeping it fresh, running through it over and over, it may impact your entire day. You may snap at your partner or coworkers, leaving them to wonder what they did to make you so angry.

Alternatively, if you raised your sons never to talk back or stray from perfect manners, you would almost certainly judge the boys on the elevator harshly—and not only them, but their parents too, for doing such a poor job raising them. The incident might launch you on a mental tirade against the moral failures of society. *What's the world coming to when children feel free to insult adults?* You generalize the incident to affirm your own virtues while condemning others.

If you've just come from eating a messy lunch, you might think the boys spotted a stray bit of food on your clothing. If it's a windy day, you might wonder if your hair got mussed. If coming from a job interview that went poorly, perhaps they sense your defeat and find it amusing. In all these instances, you assume that the boys' behavior is justified by something about you.

If you're young enough to remember being ostracized in school and teased by the popular kids, the boys in the elevator might trigger those feelings in an unexpectedly powerful fashion. The old shame from your school days reasserts itself and depresses your mood for the rest of the day. If you've been mugged by two teenage boys, you may feel threatened or enraged. On the other hand, if you recall what it was like to be an adolescent—the absurd pranks you played, the stupid, obnoxious things that used to make you laugh—you may empathize with the boys and vicariously enjoy their whispered secrets. Even in a simple, time-limited interaction such as this, there are a wide variety of possible responses, and they're all determined by *past experience.*

The second example, in which your two friends exclude you, is more difficult to get past, because the relationships involved are closer and more significant. Nonetheless, your past will determine how you feel and respond. If being left out is a familiar experience for you, if other friends have abruptly and unexpectedly dumped you, the discovery of this new "infidelity" will be all the more painful. It's not just an isolated event; it's a trend, a recurring pattern, and you are much more likely to blame yourself. *Why does this keep happening to me? What am I doing wrong?*

If, on the other hand, you've never had trouble making friends and you have many other close friends, then you'll probably shrug it off and excuse the two who excluded you. It's fine if friends occasionally do things without you. Should it happen again, you're willing and able to move on. Their friendship is not essential to your well-being.

The final example, involving your brother, is far more problematic. No matter how good you feel about yourself, no matter how many successes or friends you have, if your beloved brother cuts you out of his life for no reason, you will no doubt feel devastated and bewildered. You probably can't let it go without some explanation. Maybe he's getting divorced or going bankrupt and trying to hide it from you out of embarrassment. Or perhaps he was diagnosed with a terminal illness and can't bear to face you with the news. Without some explanation, most people would get angry with their brother. The cutoff of all communication is likely to be perceived as an attack. When we feel attacked, we either defend or counterattack. Or both.

But even here, it is the past that shapes our feelings and responses. That treasured relationship with your brother? It's based in the past. You and he no longer live in the same house. It's been ages since you spent more than a day or two together. Your image of him was shaped long ago. It's a composite of fond memories from good times. The brother who has rejected you is not the same person as the brother whose image you cherish in memory. Hard as it may be to admit, it's not your relationship with your brother that you fear to lose. It's your own past, as well as its extension into the future: the hope and expectation of forming more good memories of your brother that align with and support the old ones.

*   *   *

We judge all relationships in terms of the past—always. It's where they live. By preserving the past in memory, we allow it to determine our future. The past crowds out the present, which is the only time in which we can make a real change. As *A Course in Miracles* reminds us in Workbook lessons 7 and 8, "*I see only the past*" and "*My mind is preoccupied with past thoughts.*" By keeping us in the past, the ego blocks change. But "*the past is over. It can touch me not.*"[3] So why are we so stuck? We must understand the power that we give to the past if we want to move beyond grievances and experience true forgiveness.

> *You consider it "natural" to use your past experience as the reference point from which to judge the present. Yet this is unnatural because it is delusional. When you have learned to look on everyone with no reference at all to the past, either his or yours as you perceived it, you will be able to learn from what you see now. . . .*
>
> *To be born again is to let the past go, and look without condemnation on the present. The cloud that obscures God's Son to you is the past, and if you would have it past and gone, you must not see it now. If you see it now in your illusions, it has not gone from you, although it is not there.*[4]

Understanding the relationship of grievances to the past, we are now in a position to consider the Course's core teaching on forgiveness:

> *Forgiveness recognizes that what you thought your brother did to you has not occurred. It does not pardon sins and make them real. It sees there was no sin. And in that view*

are all your sins forgiven. What is sin, except a false idea about God's Son? Forgiveness merely sees its falsity, and therefore lets it go.[5]

This is the Course's radical prescription for how to forgive. The grievances we hold against one another are for things that never occurred, because they're based on a past that never happened except in dreams.

We have forgotten that we are God's Creation, His one Son. Although our true Identity is shared, we believe that we are separate individuals. The Course can state definitively that "*what you thought your brother did to you has not occurred,*"[6] because in the eyes of God and the Holy Spirit, your brother and you are one and the same being, so how can he *do* anything to you? How can a Oneness that's eternally whole and has no separate parts attack itself? Further, *everything* that seems to occur within the world of time and space is illusion. It doesn't matter whether it belongs to the past or the future. In God's reality, which is love and only love, it never happened.

Recall those three powerful lines from the Course's Introduction, which sum up its entire teaching:

Nothing real can be threatened.
Nothing unreal exists.
Herein lies the peace of God.[7]

We cannot be hurt by what is unreal and does not exist. If we accept this fact, it becomes our task to overlook the unreal and recall only the real. Forget the ego and its deadly world of grievances and strife. Remember only what God created. Put this into practice, and it becomes a powerful tool for transformation, one that applies to every possible situation.

Selective Forgetting, Blanket Forgiving

Forgiveness is not something you *do.* Rather, it is *undoing:* a release from an illusory past that you once believed in. Nor is it forced upon you. It is a choice you make, a choice for peace. Once chosen, you don't even have to *do* the undoing. That's the Holy Spirit's job. "*Correction is not your function.*"[8] You don't know how to go about it. Your part is merely to allow the undoing—to be willing to let the Holy Spirit show you another way of seeing and not get in the way. "*I need do nothing except not to interfere.*"[9] How do you interfere? By siding with the ego and choosing grievances *in any form* over love. Make one exception, hold back any aspect of your life, and you've signed on to the ego's plan for "salvation" once again.

The ego's plan, as we've seen, is to hold grievances. It carries out this plan through selective memory. It remembers the people and events that affronted you, frightened you, angered or embarrassed you. It prioritizes what went wrong over what went right.

The Holy Spirit uses a different set of criteria for selecting memories. He focuses only on what is real and what will lead you to experience that reality. All else falls by the wayside. You don't need to get rid of those negative memories or deny them in any way. You simply shed them along with the rest of the nonexistent past. This process is essential to forgiveness as prescribed by the Course.

> *To forgive is merely to remember only the loving thoughts you gave in the past, and those that were given you. All the rest must be forgotten. Forgiveness is a selective remembering, based not on your selection.*[10]

We remember only loving thoughts because only those are true: they are the only ones that comport with the truth of our Identity as God created it. All else is part of the ego's grand delusion. The Holy Spirit does not credit them in any way, because for Him they do not exist and never did. This is why He is in charge of the selection process and not you. He sees what's real; you do not. You must learn to deny the unreal before you can see truly, as He does.

According to the Course, this is the constructive use of denial, as opposed to the unhelpful psychological defense mechanism that goes by the same name. When *we* employ denial as a defense, what we deny continues to exist. We have already acknowledged its reality, but because it is so threatening, we push it out of awareness and deny that it exists.

I've witnessed this sort of denial applied to everything from having my car towed (*Where did it go? I'm sure I parked it right here*) to cancer (*Did the doctor really say that? I don't think so*) to a spouse's infidelity (*He wouldn't do that. I refuse to believe it*). Psychologists consider denial to be a very primitive defense mechanism, because it is so all-or-nothing and because it can reshape fact into fantasy. More damagingly still, as we saw with the leaky roof in part 1, once a threat is denied, we won't do anything to correct it. If it doesn't exist for us, then what is there to be dealt with?

The Course tells us that we use psychological denial all the time to reject the presence of God and our true Self because these are threatening to the ego. What we need to do instead is "*to deny the denial of truth*."[11]

> *[Deny] the ability of anything not of God to affect you. This is the proper use of denial. It is not used to hide anything, but to correct error. . . . True denial is a powerful protective device. You can and should deny any belief that error can hurt you. This kind of denial is not a concealment but a correction.*[12]

The Holy Spirit does this for us when He selects out only those elements of the past that are loving and denies the reality of everything else.

You might think of the Holy Spirit as a filter that you apply to your perception and interpretation of people and events, or like polarizing sunglasses that remove the glare that interferes with vision. He filters out every unloving thought or deed, every perception that's not aligned with your true Self. None of them make it through to contaminate the present moment. The attack thoughts and past memories that He strains out are no more. They were never real. All that remains is the pure, clear vision of your brother seen as he truly is: the Christ, the Son of God. Remember, without the past there can be no grievances. This is why the Course can state that "*the present* is *forgiveness*."[13] In the present moment—purified of the past, unchained from the future—only love remains.

Another helpful metaphor is to think of the Holy Spirit and forgiveness as a universal solvent: a perfect cleaning solution capable of dissolving anything that does not come from love. Apply several drops of it to any difficult situation whatsoever, and watch the stain of conflict fade and disappear. Take those whose angry scowls and furrowed frowns have troubled you in the past, let them soak for a while in a bath of pure liquid forgiveness, and behold! They emerge with only radiant smiles. Nothing can withstand the power of this miraculous universal solvent. We could say that forgiveness is the Holy Spirit's "solution" to all of your problems.

12

Forgiving the Unforgivable

We have seen how grievances keep the past alive. This is true not only for the personal past, but for the collective past as well. Some of the most hardened grievances are based on cultural or historical memories of events that occurred long ago, events that never touched us personally, but which are nevertheless expressed as toxic prejudices stretching across the centuries.

When I visited the island of Crete in the 1980s I heard a story about a German who had been stationed there as a soldier during World War II. He'd returned decades later on holiday to revisit his fond memories of the island. His body was found murdered. Someone remembered him, not as he was in the present, an innocent tourist, but in the role he had played during the war. That grievance from the past proved fatal.

I know Jews who refuse to visit Germany because of the Holocaust, even though almost eighty years have passed and Germany has done far more to come to terms with its dark past than its neighbors Austria and Switzerland. During the Bosnian-Kosovo war of 1992–95, Serbian Christians inflamed prejudices that had lain dormant since the thirteenth century, leading to violence and genocide against Muslims with whom they had lived side by side for hundreds of years.

"Christ-Killer"

These historical or collective grievances attach themselves to an entire group of people, who stand accused of an unforgivable crime they allegedly committed in the past. One of the most enduring and destructive of these is the calumny according to which the Jewish people bear responsibility for the crucifixion of Jesus—that in urging Pilate to crucify him, they willingly called this curse down upon their people for all generations to come. It provided the original justification for anti-Semitism and even today far too many Christians still subscribe to it, even though historians have debunked it as a lie.

My grandfather had his own scary childhood encounter with the pernicious lie that the Jews killed Jesus. He had grown up in Russia under the tsars, a place and time notorious for its oppression of Jews. Entire villages were massacred in anti-Semitic pogroms justified by falsehoods like the "blood libel" that Jews murdered Christian children and used their blood to make the Passover matzo.

My grandfather's childhood nickname was Borki, short for Boris. He was only about eight or nine years old when, walking home through town one day, he was jumped by a gang of older boys, who taunted him and shouted that he was a "Christ-killer." They punched him, shoved him to the ground, and kicked at him. He could have been seriously injured, except that this incident happened to take place in front of a Russian Orthodox church. A priest, hearing the shouts and curses, came running out of the church into the street to break up the fight. He asked the boys what had happened. Why were they attacking this younger boy? They replied, "He's a Christ-killer! Borki is a Christ-killer!" He looked at the boys, then asked one of them, "Did *you* see Borki kill Christ?" The boy shook his head. Obviously he hadn't. The priest turned to the next boy and asked the same question. To each one he asked, "Did *you* see Borki kill Christ?" Each was forced to admit that, no, in fact he had not. They had no evidence whatsoever that Borki was implicated in this crime. "So why do you call him Christ-killer?" the priest asked.

The priest went on to explain the ancient roots of Judaism and how Christianity itself grew out of it. The boys apologized (in my imagination, they are all teary-eyed) and never again troubled my grandfather. He returned home that day with some bruises and with deep respect and gratitude for the wise, compassionate priest who'd come to his rescue.

My grandfather was an unusually accepting and generous man. He had no enemies that I knew of, and I rarely heard criticism about anyone from his lips. I wonder now whether this incident might have played a role in shaping such a forgiving attitude. If so, then that priest's intervention affected thousands of others my grandfather encountered over the course of his life, including me. Perhaps I would not be writing a book on relationships and forgiveness were it not for the actions of an anonymous Russian Orthodox priest on that day long ago in the early years of the twentieth century.

My grandfather's experience offers a good example of how a centuries-old grievance against an entire people, brought to bear against one young boy, can be released. By virtue of his authority, the priest could compel the attackers to stop and listen to him. He gently led them to examine their prejudice and to realize that it had nothing to do with them or my grandfather. It was not based on present fact but past fiction. None of the boys had witnessed Borki killing Christ; they knew full well that an eight-year-old Jewish boy in Russia had nothing to do with events that had occurred almost two millennia earlier in the Middle East. The priest also introduced new information about the nature of Judaism and its relation to Christianity. And so, in this one instance at least, a collective grievance against an entire people was undone.

Perhaps the boys incorporated the priest's lesson and carried it with them lifelong, passing it along to others as well. At least that's my hope. If so, then for them, an imaginary past that never occurred, in which the Jews were eternally guilty of a crime beyond repentance, was recognized as a lie and dispelled. A centuries-old grievance gave way to forgiveness. *What you thought your brother did to you has not occurred.*

The Holocaust as Grievance

Regarding the Jews and Jesus, there was never any justification for holding a grievance against an entire religion. The ancient Jews had committed no crime. But let's turn to a more recent example, one that also involves the Jewish people: the Holocaust, in which the Nazis systematically exterminated six million European Jews. Had they triumphed in World War II, there is little doubt that they would have wiped out the entire Jewish people, or come very close to it. How do you go about forgiving something like that? Especially for those Jews who lost entire branches of their families?

Recall those Jews who to this day refuse to visit Germany? Rationally, they know that no German born after 1935 can reasonably bear responsibility for the Holocaust. But to those who refuse forgiveness, such details don't matter. The sins of the fathers are counted against the sons, so the German people as a whole stand accused of a crime that few of them can even remember. Yet isn't this the same kind of thinking that made Jews Christ-killers and led to the attack on Borki? Collective grievances are not confined to any one country or group. Our refusal to forgive makes perpetrators of us all.

A closely related question—one that's frequently asked in Course study groups when the topic of forgiveness comes up—is, "How can you possibly forgive Hitler?" This simply takes the Holocaust and gives it a personal face. We refuse to forgive Hitler because of his direct responsibility for countless suffering and millions of deaths.

The fact that this question comes up so often reveals something important about the way we commonly view forgiveness. We believe that it's conditioned upon the crime: that there is a hierarchy of evil in which some crimes are forgivable, perhaps even most, but certain crimes, like genocide, are so heinous that they stand beyond anyone's capacity to forgive.

But what exactly qualifies them as unforgivable? The number of lives lost? The degree of suffering inflicted? How do we begin to measure and quantify those things? Where do you draw the line? Whether it's six million or "only" six killed, someone is still left deeply hurting.

When we judge anything as unforgivable, that's *our* judgment, not the Holy Spirit's. The power of forgiveness lies in its universal applicability, and this in turn rests on a vision of holiness that goes well beyond our familiar notions of self and other. To the Holy Spirit there is no "other"; the concept makes no sense. All are one, and so all are forgiven the "sin" of separation and its dark consequences. The moment we carve out an exception to this and judge anyone as unforgivable—even someone whose deeds were as despicable as Hitler's—we are affirming the ego over the Holy Spirit. We choose the dream over awakening. And the accusing finger that points in the direction of the other will inevitably convict us as well, because we are one.

American Genocide

This lesson is powerfully illustrated in a story I once heard from the Czech psychiatrist and psychedelic researcher Stan Grof, MD, which he recounts in his wonderful autobiography, *When the Impossible Happens.*[1] Early in his career Stan had read that the Native American Church made use of the peyote cactus (source of the psychedelic compound mescaline) as a sacrament in their rituals. He was very interested in attending such a ceremony, and, as these things often go, met and became friendly with a fellow psychiatrist who was a Native American. In short order, Stan and several members of his team found themselves headed out to the Great Plains of Kansas to join members of the Potawatomi tribe for a ritual peyote ceremony.

Although they had been invited by the tribal leader, it was a requirement that each participant in the ritual had to formally accept them into the circle before the ceremony could begin. This involved a lot of questioning. and in the process strong feelings emerged on the part of the Native Americans about the white race and the lies, forced migrations, and slaughter they had perpetrated on the Native American tribes. Eventually all of the Potawatomi accepted their white guests and welcomed them to the circle—except for one man. His hatred for the white race was palpable; it radiated from him in waves. His fellows prevailed upon him to allow the ceremony to go forward, but he made it clear by his angry demeanor that he was not a willing participant. He considered the white man's presence in such a sacred setting a violation. Stan felt that the anger that blazed from this man's eyes was personally directed at him. It contaminated the ceremony and made the whole experience extremely uncomfortable.

Toward the end of the ceremony, one of Stan's associates acknowledged the devastation wrought on the Native

Americans by the European colonizers. He also expressed feelings of sympathy for Stan, who was so far from his homeland in Czechoslovakia. In the space of an instant, the recalcitrant man's demeanor changed. His resentment vanished, and he threw himself at Stan's feet, sobbing inconsolably for perhaps twenty minutes. He explained how he had regarded Stan and all the other whites at the ceremony as intruders and enemies of his people. But as a visitor from Czechoslovakia, Stan had played no role in the devastation of the Native Americans; he was innocent of those crimes.

The man's remorse had still deeper roots. He confessed that he had been drafted into the Air Force during World War II and in the final days of the war had participated in the totally unnecessary bombing of a Czech city. As it turned out, *he* was the perpetrator and Stan the victim. He had bombed and wrought destruction on Stan's people, not the other way around, as he'd believed. He apologized for his behavior and begged everyone's forgiveness. He shared his newfound insight that there would be no hope for the world if we all carried the grievances of our ancestors down from one generation to the next.

Stan's story powerfully illustrates a truth about human nature. We have all cast ourselves as victims of violence at some point in our lives, and yet are we not all perpetrators as well? Under the ego's dominion, who among us has not hurt someone, even if unintentionally? Even if only in our thoughts and fantasies?

The ego attacks. That is its nature. Usually the attack is covert, because no one really feels good about attacking and most prefer not to be seen that way. But occasionally it erupts into full, ugly view, exposing the ego's viciousness.

To the extent that we identify with the ego and see ourselves as bodies vying for scarce resources, clamoring for our own precious slice of specialness, attack becomes inevitable, loss unavoidable, and grievances a natural outcome. That's how the ego sees it. In its zero-sum-game world there are no winners. We are all sinners guilty of many crimes and deserving of the death penalty we will one day receive.

The alternative view, the Holy Spirit's, is that we are sinless, invulnerable to attack and loss, because that's how God created us. There is no compromise in this. Either we are pure, perfect love, unified in the one Self that God created, or we are monsters hell-bent on grabbing what little we can, where we can, and from whomever we can (all the while smiling in false innocence).

The point of view that you subscribe to in any given moment is what you'll see reflected in the world, in others, and of course in yourself. Are you pardoned for your perceived sins by virtue of what you are, or damned by them because of what you believe you are? Are you the Christ, the holy Son of God? Or something else—something incomplete, fragmented, and painfully vulnerable? That's the choice that confronts you. All your relationships will reflect that choice and will be patterned accordingly.

Original Guilt
In Stan Grof's story, the Native American man who was resentful of all whites was harboring a massive grievance.

He refused to look at this in the discussion before the peyote ceremony, and he carried it through the shared psychedelic experience. He felt righteous, justified in his anger, and he used this as a wedge to pry himself apart from the group.

Even so, such a gathering sets a powerful intention for healing. Stan provided the means for that healing simply by his presence. He became a target for centuries of accumulated rage. But this vanished the moment the man learned that Stan was from another country and could have had nothing to do with the white's persecution of his ancestors.

Had this man been willing to examine his grievance more closely, he wouldn't have needed a visitor from Czechoslovakia to bring him to this realization. Not one person in that peyote circle had done anything to harm him, his family, or his people. Like Borki, Stan and his colleagues were innocent. When the truth finally emerged, it turned the tables and exposed this man as the only real killer among them.

Behind all of his anger, and no doubt fueling it, there lay a massive load of guilt for the cruel bombing in which he'd participated. In psychological terms, he had *projected* his guilt outward onto the entire white race such that *he* became the victim while *they* were the ones guilty of a crime against humanity. He was spared from having to feel the guilt and shame of what he'd done during the war by covering it over with righteous rage.

In the same way, we all project the original guilt and shame of the separation onto our brothers and sisters. *We* didn't do anything; *they* did! The mere fact that others appear to us as separate is itself a silent accusation. Each body we encounter becomes that accusing finger pointing back in our direction. The guilt we projected onto them engenders fear of attack—from them, but also from God—and this in turn leads to counterattack justified in the name of self-defense. Around and around it goes. This cycle of grievances would have no end were it not for the Holy Spirit.

The Holiest Spot on Earth

The story of Stan Grof and the Potawatomi tribesman demonstrates the remarkable byways taken by the Holy Spirit to bring about forgiveness and healing. The path that would seem most direct and obvious is not always the most effective. As with hitting bottom, often we need to experience the ego's obstinacy before we're finally willing to let go and forgive.

The Potawatomi man could have expressed his anger and hurt prior to the ceremony and arrived at a happy resolution. Likewise, the communal joining under the influence of the peyote could have brought him to a powerful sense of completion. But his stubborn, smoldering rage and its total release in the space of a single moment of insight provided him and the others with a far more powerful experience.

No one planned for it to happen this way. There was no choreographed moment when the white visitors raised their hands to make it known that one of them was not in fact an American and therefore not implicitly guilty of

genocide. Rather it was a by-product of the deep unconscious intention for healing that lives in all of us. Perhaps
this surfaced through the influence of the peyote. Perhaps
it was the result of the Potawatomi allowing whites into
their sacred circle. Or perhaps it was just the right time. It
doesn't matter. At some level, the willingness to forgive was
present and that was enough.

Grof and the Potawatomi encountered a true healing
that day. Attack gave way to a complete, unconditional
surrender into forgiveness. Not one vestige of this man's
rage remained, nor could it ever return again. Having been
forced to look in the mirror and behold his own guilt,
he'd grasped that unforgiving rage of the kind he'd felt
was never justified toward anyone. Attack begets attack.
Those who live by the sword will just as surely die by the
sword. In the end, as we have seen, the one most injured
is yourself.

In one of its most beautiful and inspiring passages, the
Course says this about such healing:

> *The blood of hatred fades to let the grass grow green again,
> and let the flowers be all white and sparkling in the summer
> sun. What was a place of death has now become a living
> temple in a world of light. . . .*
>
> *The holiest of all the spots on earth is where an ancient
> hatred has become a present love. . . . There is no place in
> Heaven holier. . . . What hatred has released to love becomes
> the brightest light in Heaven's radiance. And all the lights
> in Heaven brighter grow, in gratitude for what has been
> restored.*[2]

A shrine to holiness sprang into being that day on the sweeping Great Plains of America, a shrine very different from the other monuments commemorating bloody battles and strife. This shrine needs no statues, plaques, or visitor center, because its true home is to be found in the mind. We are all more peaceful, less likely to succumb to the temptation of attack, because of what one man was willing to face in himself that day—for his own healing and for that of the world. He forgave his brother Stan, and he forgave himself in the recognition that there is no difference. Such is the path of salvation.

13

Time to Forgive

Bill Thetford, the coscribe of *A Course in Miracles*, was once asked, "How do you know whether or not you're making progress with the Course?" Bill answered with his own question: *how long does it take you to forgive a grievance?*

Forgiveness seems difficult, but really it requires no time at all. How long does it take to change your mind—to shift the way you see things in order to release the past and recognize that what you thought your brother did to you *has not occurred*? It can happen in a single moment of insight, as it did with the Potawatomi man. So the real question becomes, how long does it take before you are *willing* to acknowledge your grievance, bring it into awareness, and set an intention to let it go? How much time must pass and how much hurt and anger must you endure before you're willing to replace your interpretation of what happened with the Holy Spirit's?

In my book *From Plagues to Miracles*, I wrote about a woman I once treated in psychotherapy who spent session after session boiling over with rage about an episode of sexual abuse from her childhood. She would describe in grisly detail her violent revenge fantasies while I sat patiently listening. The things she imagined doing to the man who abused her could hardly be considered forgiving. As a Course student, I was well aware of this. Yet I did not try to stop her or correct her and make her wrong. I understood that in order to heal, she needed to express her rage. She needed to experience the sense of empowerment she gained from those fantasies, and she could only do so in the safe space of my office. They were reverberations of the violence done to her, which she had to purge from her mind. How could she bring them forth for healing without feeling them fully?

Over time this woman's rage cooled and burned itself out, as any great fire will do. The fantasies lost their intensity. They were no longer compelling or satisfying, because they were no longer needed. The purpose they'd served had been met. Months later, I checked in with her about this episode of abuse. She no longer felt enraged. In fact, her feelings about it were rather bland. It had happened, it was painful, and it was over. Her abuser had died many years before our therapy began. Why resurrect him and waste her time by giving him a second thought? It had taken her years to release this grievance, understandable as it was. Her path to forgiveness had run through the valley of hatred and violence. But it had worked. She had done it. She had let her grievance go.

Too often in Course study groups, I have witnessed judgments leveled against those who, for whatever reason, were unable to turn on a dime and instantly forgive. Other members would try to persuade them that they really should forgive now, as if their unwillingness or inability to forgive were wrong. Perhaps their refusal somehow called into question the commitment of the other group members, or perhaps it undermined for them the power of the Course's teaching, and these things became the source of a new grievance targeted against the one who could not forgive. We need to forgive those who are not yet able to forgive, because we don't know the best path to forgiveness for them. We don't know whether that should take place in an instant or over a lifetime.

The purpose of time, when used by the Holy Spirit, is to *give us time* to change our mind and find our way to forgiveness. Whether that requires minutes or millennia is not up to us. That's not a judgment we're fit to make. No one on this earth can know the best path to healing for anyone else. We leave that to the Holy Spirit. If we try to step in and assume His role in an attempt to speed forgiveness along, then we're really saying that we don't trust Him. We believe that we can do it better. What but the ego would make this claim?

How do you respond when the grievance is not yours, but someone else's? For example, if someone is upset with you for no reason that you can figure out, or if you know you're being falsely accused, but they refuse to hear your explanations. Is it *your* fault that they're holding a grievance against you? Must you live with that burden? How are we supposed to react in such situations?

First, you need to recognize the temptation to hold a countergrievance of your own. If the other person hates you, you feel free to hate them back—in fact your hate is justified, because you didn't start this war. This kind of thinking does not lead to forgiveness. Much better to refrain from trying to shove forgiveness down their throats and instead tend to your own unforgiving thoughts. Be vigilant against the ego's need to justify its existence through attack. If they're upset with you, you won't quell their anger by adding your own to the mix. Anger is contagious. Its seeds blow everywhere and take root like stubborn, noxious weeds. Don't let them. Visualize the other person's attacks against you as if they were a baited hook. Bite down on that hook, and now both of you are caught up in grievances and in need of forgiveness. You can't help them escape their anger by getting hooked yourself.

On the other hand, you can use their grievance against you to remind yourself of who you really are and what you really want. You can become all the more determined not to judge them or respond in kind. How? By handing off the situation and your feelings about it to the Holy Spirit. "*Take this from me and look upon it, judging it for me. . . . Teach me how* not *to make of it an obstacle to peace, but let You use it for me, to facilitate its coming.*"[1]

You can't possibly know what's driving the other person's behavior, so there's no point in trying to figure it out. Let the Holy Spirit take charge. Don't try to tell Him what the outcome should be or how you think He should get there. Let it go completely. Trust that in some way, at some deep level, the other person will benefit, even if you never see any signs of it. *"It does not matter if another thinks your gifts [of forgiveness] unworthy. In his mind there is a part that joins with yours in thanking you."*[2] By remaining committed to your own forgiveness, you make it all the more likely that the other person will find their way to it too.

*   *   *

Bill Thetford became the target of someone else's grievance while he and Helen were scribing the Course in the 1960s. He had a colleague in the psychology department at Columbia, a man named Arthur with whom he'd been very friendly, until one day Arthur simply stopped speaking to him. Bill suspected this had something to do with Helen. Whenever Bill entered any room, Arthur would ignore him, acting as though he didn't even exist. Nor did Arthur make any effort to be subtle about it. Bill could have gotten angry. He could have confronted Arthur. He could have shunned him in kind. But instead Bill decided to make Arthur his first experiment in applying the Course's principles of forgiveness.

Every morning Bill would enter Arthur's office, take a chair opposite Arthur's desk, and simply sit there with him. The moment Bill entered, Arthur would tent his newspaper in front of his face and hide behind it. Despite this, Bill remained peaceful. He would meditate on the Course while Arthur pretended he wasn't there. This went on for weeks. One morning, however, Bill had a conflicting obligation and didn't show up in Arthur's office. Arthur wondered where he could be. Out of concern that something bad might have happened, Arthur went looking for him. This opened a door, and they began to speak again. But that was not the end of it.

Months later the two men were attending a professional conference together. Their hotel was overbooked, and the conference participants were asked to pair up and share rooms if possible. Arthur approached Bill to ask if they might room together. "You're the only one here I want to be with," he said. Before dinner, they got drinks at the bar. At one point, Arthur reached over and plucked six almonds from the snack bowl, sliding three toward Bill and keeping three for himself.

"Edgar Cayce told me that if you eat three almonds a day, you won't get cancer," he explained.

Bill almost fell off his barstool. Bill not only knew about Cayce and held him in high regard, he had already met with his son, Hugh Lynn, whose opinion he and Helen had sought out regarding the early scribing of the Course. (They would later give Hugh Lynn a review copy of their first completed draft.) And now here was Arthur—Bill's peer and, like him, a respected academic psychologist—quoting Cayce!

As it turned out, Arthur had known Edgar Cayce personally. He had lunched at Cayce's house on Sundays while stationed in the Navy near Cayce's home in Virginia Beach. For Bill, this hidden connection with Edgar Cayce served as further confirmation that the grievance between them had been healed and that forgiveness as taught by *A Course in Miracles* really did work. He and Arthur never had problems again.

Bill spent the last years of his life applying forgiveness to all of his significant relationships from the past. He completed this work shortly before his death in 1988. As a result, for Bill, death was a leap into freedom. As if to highlight the point, and with his characteristic sense of humor, Bill left his body on July 4—Independence Day.

For Bill and Arthur, the forgiveness process played out over many months. Why? Because that was the most effective path for their level of readiness. Nevertheless, when we jettison our judgments and let the Holy Spirit take charge, without hesitation or doubt, forgiveness can leap across the barrier of years and take place in no time at all. Judy Skutch Whitson, one of the founders of the Foundation for Inner Peace, gives this wonderful example.

Judy was born and raised in a Jewish household. Although the Course has been her spiritual path since it first came into her life in May 1975, she continued to observe the Jewish holidays and identify as a Jew. Her father was a leader in Jewish communal life. When she began working with the Course, she was less than comfortable with some of its strongly Christian language.

Interestingly, her father had no problem with this once he grasped the metaphysics behind the Christian terminology. Other family members were not so understanding. An entire set of aunts and cousins on her father's side chose to view her public involvement with the Course as a repudiation of her father's Judaism. They decided to eliminate her from their lives. Judy found this painful, but there was nothing she could do to change their minds, so she reluctantly accepted the situation. This went on not for a few months but for decades.

Like Bill, Judy was intent on healing all of her unforgiven relationships. She and her daughter, Tam, were practicing the Workbook lessons together with the goal of shining a light on all areas of unforgiveness. Judy was by this time in her mid-eighties; who knew how many years she had left? She decided she would focus on her estranged family.

She hadn't spoken to those relatives in ages. Tam reminded her that she didn't need to reach out to them. Not a word need ever be spoken. All Judy had to do was forgive them *in her own mind*. That would be enough. And what time was better suited than right now? Judy agreed: yes, it was time.

They sat together with closed eyes, and Judy completely let go of the past. Her aunts' and cousins' bitter judgments, the guilt she had felt about disappointing them, the decades of silence and distance—she was willing to forgive everything. The past was over, so why not release it? What could be simpler? She opened her eyes feeling much lighter and expecting nothing more to come of it. She'd done her part and forgiven her perception of her estranged relatives. As Tam had reminded her, that was indeed enough.

About twenty minutes later, Judy received an email. It was from one of her cousins. He had contacted her because he wanted to invite her and her husband, Whit, to his mother's hundredth birthday party. This began a loving correspondence, and the other family members joined in. The antagonism of the intervening decades was nowhere to be found. It had vanished in an instant, as if it had never been. And maybe it hadn't. Once Judy chose to forgive, the past truly was over. With no further effort on her part, her decision was reflected in the outer world and rippled out to her family. Recall again the Course's definition of forgiveness:

> *Forgiveness recognizes what you thought your brother did to you has not occurred. It does not pardon sins and make them real. It sees there was no sin. And in that view are all your sins forgiven.*[3]

The Course also tells us in Workbook lesson 336, "*Forgiveness lets me know that minds are joined.*" Judy's release of the past extended to the mind of her cousin and brought forgiveness to him as well. As a result, the rift between them was not just ended, it effectively had never occurred.

In Workbook lesson 292 the Course promises, "*A happy outcome to all things is sure.*" The only variable is how many moments of illusory time we allow to stand between us and that happy outcome. How many precious instants do we waste in pursuit of ego-driven goals? We do have a choice. We can delay salvation, or we can embrace it. We can forgive our grievances and dissolve them, or we can prolong them and keep both ourselves and others miserable for a bit longer. In every moment, the choice is ours. But once made, the past and its consequences are indeed over. "*For what can be forgiven but the past, and if it is forgiven it is gone.*"[4]

14

Shadows and Mirrors: Relationships as Reflections of Self

Projection is a cornerstone of the ego's approach to relationships. We touched on it earlier, but now we must examine it more closely.

Projection is a psychological defense mechanism, similar to denial, in which we escape from what we find unacceptable in ourselves by projecting it outward onto others. We then react to them and their "sins" by attacking them, without apparent threat to our own psychological well-being.

A good example of this is homophobia. Those most biased against gays are likely to be the ones struggling mightily against their own homosexual impulses. But as we've seen, defenses do not solve the problem. They keep it alive. "*It is essential to realize that all defenses* do *what they would defend. . . . What they defend is placed in them for safe-keeping, and as they operate they bring it to you.*"[1]

The crusader against gay rights spends a great deal of time thinking about gays.

We cannot undo our "sins" by outsourcing them to someone else and then judging that person for what belongs to *us*. Shame cannot be alleviated by trying to make another feel more shameful. It will remain with us and it will grow stronger in them.

In part 1, we saw that to be free of shame it was necessary to identify and acknowledge its presence within us and then to expose what we'd kept hidden. Projection is a bit more complicated. We can't acknowledge what we projected out without first taking it back and owning it. The moment this occurs, the projection is undone and healing can occur, as with the Potawatomi man. The target of projection can now be seen for who and what it really is and always was: the wholly innocent Son of God.

Whereas shame primarily affects the perception of self, projection takes this a step further and distorts our perception of others. Projection is not simply a defense mechanism to protect you from what you'd rather not have to face in yourself; it is an attack on reality. By locating the source of a grievance outside yourself, in another person, you block any chance of exposing it for the fiction that it is. You've hidden it where it can no longer be brought forth, because you think it no longer lives within you. It's not about *you* anymore; it's about *them*. This keeps you and them apart. They are *not* like you. They will *never* be a *thou*. They are *other*—something different, deserving of your judgment, your rejection, and your attack. Projection not only preserves but strengthens the ego's world of separation.

> *Projection and attack are inevitably related, because projection is always a means of justifying attack. Anger without projection is impossible. The ego uses projection only to destroy your perception of both yourself and your brothers. The process begins by excluding something that exists in you but which you do not want, and leads directly to excluding you from your brothers.*[2]

Projection tries to get rid of what's not wanted by pretending it can be split off from the self and relocated in the other. As a result, each use of projection further fragments the world. It is the opposite of *tikkun olam*.

Behold your projections in another, and you blind yourself to who they really are. You'll see the projection, not the person behind it. You'll form a grievance based on that projection without ever having to acknowledge its source in your own mind.

Project *anything* onto *anyone*, and you lose sight of their reality. You no longer know them, nor do you care to. You become incapable of beholding the Christ in them. Wherever you look, you see only bits and pieces of your own twisted, fragmented self. It's like a fun-house hall of mirrors—only without the fun. The projections of your own worst impulses surround you everywhere. They distort your perception of yourself and crowd out your ability to see anyone or anything else clearly.

These projections can grow extremely threatening, and indeed intolerable. At this point we explode in anger and lash out at the object of our projection. One of my psychotherapy mentors liked to say that anger is nothing more than a hurt that we've decided will never go away. Rather than facing that hurt, owning it, and beginning the healing process, we project it away from us onto another. But once it is projected, it must remain with us.

How do we find our way out of the ego's no-fun house? How do we escape from this dizzying maze of projections and reflections of our own worst nature? We begin by taking note of those things that irritate us most in others and assume that they are our own projections; otherwise why would we be so triggered? Having identified them, we can search for their origins in our own thoughts and behavior.

Do other people strike you as angry? Do you judge them for it? Then look for the seeds of anger within yourself. Are you infuriated by greedy rich people who only seem to care about accumulating wealth? Then look for those hidden pockets of greed in yourself. Where have you behaved greedily toward others? It may not necessarily involve money. Try to identify situations in which you intentionally withheld what you could have easily given or where you wanted a certain outcome and went after it, not caring how that might affect others. Alternatively, perhaps you struggle with money, barely scraping by. You secretly envy rich people and wish you could be one of them, but outwardly you resent them.

Once you identify the source of your projection, you have an opportunity to take it back. But this is not easy to do from within the hall of mirrors, where you see your "sins" reflected outward in everyone but yourself. Remember, the "original sin" is the separation. The body is the ego's "proof" that the separation was real, and bodies surround you everywhere. Their very presence testifies to your guilt about what you think you did to God and His Son. In order to take back your projections and escape from the ego's hall of mirrors, you will once again need help. You'll need a guide who is not distracted or confused by these bodies, these myriad reflections of guilt: a guide who sees through the façade to the holiness beneath and can lead you there. That of course would be the Holy Spirit.

The Holy Spirit's task, as always, is to reverse the errors introduced into your thought system by the separation and maintained by ego. The Holy Spirit sees perfection—perfect love—and only that. He extends this equally to you and to everyone else. In this way He brings about the reversal of projection.

> *The Holy Spirit begins by perceiving you as perfect. Knowing this perfection is shared He recognizes it in others, thus strengthening it in both. Instead of anger this arouses love for both, because it establishes inclusion.*[3]

Whereas projection introduced divisions, Love undoes them by uniting us in its oneness. Because Love has no parts or aspects, it is the perfect unifier. In fact, it is the only thing that truly binds us together as one. In this sense it can be said that our brothers and sisters are either the Son of God or a body; either they are One or the "other." With love we are one; absent it, we are divided, and our sisters and brothers will seem alien and dangerous.

The Holy Spirit undoes projection because He does not see *anything* that's *unwanted*. For Him, such a category does not exist. He sees only your holiness, your innocence, your perfection, and nothing else. Nothing else is real for Him.

The Holy Spirit undoes projection by showing us our divine perfection in place of "sin," and unity instead of division. The holiness of our brothers and sisters is no longer hidden from us behind toxic projections. We join with them in the all-inclusive Love from which we were created. By undoing projection at its source, in your mind, the Holy Spirit also reverses the fragmentation it induced. His vision extends sinlessness from one mind to another and unites them in the light of holiness.

You might think of the Holy Spirit as an autocorrect function for the ego's world of judgments and grievances. Each time you make the error of judging a brother or sister as sinful, each time you choose to focus on differences rather than on sharing, each time you project your fears or shame outward in the form of attack and feel justified in counterattack, the Holy Spirit gently erases your error and overwrites it with truth. Where you beheld sin and grievances, He shows you innocence and holiness. He whites out your error and writes in the Word of God.

At first you have to consciously select this autocorrect feature. You recognize that you've made a mistake, because you're not at peace, and you directly ask the Holy Spirit to help correct your misperception: "Help me to see this differently." You may need to repeat this many times in many different circumstances, but eventually the process becomes easier and almost automatic. You come to rely on Him to autocorrect your mistaken judgments the moment they occur.

This autocorrect feature is already a part of your mind's operating system. The Holy Spirit was "installed" the instant you thought the separation real, but you have not activated this feature. You activate it by asking His help to overwrite *all* of your errors with truth. That is the practice of forgiveness.

Under the Holy Spirit's loving guidance, we no longer wander dazed and confused in the ego's hall of mirrors, slamming up against our reflected selves and accusing them of attack. We begin to awaken to the truth: that those distorted reflections, when cleansed of our projections, are identical to us. They are accurate reflections—not of our sins, but of the light and love we share. When we awaken fully, we will discover that they *are* us—there never were any mirrors or reflections except in the mind that dreamed itself separate. Now we release these false images back to oneness and reunite in the love that is our true Self, the Christ, the holy Son of God.

The Groundhog and Its Shadow

Swiss psychiatrist Carl Jung coined the term the *shadow* to describe those aspects of the self that we cannot tolerate in our conscious minds. The shadow comprises all that we have disowned and chosen to keep hidden, all that we refuse to bring forth for healing. This includes shame and guilt as well as other unacceptable feelings, such as jealousy, hatred, and rage.

Unless we acknowledge the shadow and face it in ourselves, we will project it outward onto others. But as we've seen, defense mechanisms actually do the very thing they were intended to prevent. Therefore projection is not an effective mechanism for insulating us from our shadow. On the contrary, it shows up everywhere, insistently reminding us of what we tried to banish.

Detached from its source, the shadow can be terrifying. Our own darkest impulses loom large and now appear to threaten us from without. So we attack our projected shadow as if it were some alien thing that had nothing to do with us. Because attack is not possible without projection, we might think of attack as a form of shadowboxing. We fight our own shadow, which we've projected onto others. But if you strike out and try to punch your shadow, you won't hurt it. Instead you'll smash your fist into the wall on which it was projected. You might bruise your knuckles or break some bones, but your shadow will remain intact and unharmed.

You don't destroy a shadow by attacking it. The attempt will only hurt you, because the shadow is part of you and must be faced. As the wise magician, Prospero, said in Shakespeare's *The Tempest* when confronted with the actions of his creature, Caliban, "This thing of darkness I acknowledge mine."[4] The way to dispel your shadow is to acknowledge it, and then to shine a light on it.

In the United States, February 2 is Groundhog Day. It's based on a folk myth that on this date the groundhog emerges briefly from its long winter's hibernation and stumbles outside into the cold. If the day is sunny, the groundhog sees its shadow, which scares it and drives it underground back into hibernation, guaranteeing six more weeks of winter. On the other hand, if the day is overcast, the groundhog casts no shadow. It remains aboveground, signaling that spring is just around the corner.

Whatever the holiday's merits as a forecaster of spring, it offers a useful parable regarding the shadow. Let's begin by looking closely into the nature of shadows. What are they? How do they come about?

First, a shadow has no tangible existence. Lacking in substance, it cannot be grasped or manipulated directly. It is not a thing. It is purely a matter of perception. Shadows are two-dimensional projections of darkness onto the three-dimensional world. (Plato, in the allegory of the cave in his *Republic*, postulated that this three-dimensional world is itself a shadow cast by some higher level of reality.)

Two elements are necessary to cast a shadow: a light source and something that stands in the way of that light and blocks it. Shadows, then, are a visual representation of the obstruction of light. We see them even though we cannot touch them. We also interpret them by finding some meaning in their shapes that may or may not be related to the object that gave rise to them. Hold your hand in front of a flashlight, for example, and its shadow can take the form of a dog, an alligator, a bird, or what it really is: an outspread hand with five distinct fingers.

If we want to understand the deeper meaning behind shadows, we must realize one key fact: *in order to see your own shadow, you must be facing* away *from the light.* Turn toward the light and you'll see only light, no shadow. Turn away from the light, and voilà, there's your shadow, stretching outward from your feet. Run, jump, spin—no matter what you do, your shadow remains stubbornly affixed. You cannot free yourself from it. As long as you have a physical body that blocks a light source, you will cast a shadow.

In the same way, as long as we continue to identify with the ego, which keeps us looking away from the light, we will project shadows and they will frighten us. We could think of the ego's entire world as one grand shadow play— the result of a collective turning away from the light of God in the delusional belief that we could make something better, namely, a material world that eclipses the love and light of God. But this world we made is filled with shadows, both scary and appealing, all designed to divert our attention so that we never manage to turn and look upon the holy light of the Christ Self.

The projection of your shadow onto others turns them into shadow figures as well. You no longer see them accurately. Just as the shadow of your hand might slide across another person in the shape of an alligator or dog, so does the shadow of your imaginary past creep over others, darkening and obscuring their features so they appear different and fearful to you. Your shadowy projection changes *your* perception of them, even though it does nothing to change their underlying reality as spirit. You cannot change their fundamental nature with a shadow. Remember: no shadow is real, and no shadow can hurt you. Nor can it alter the nature of the thing upon which it is projected. All shadows will vanish when brought into the light.

*   *   *

Let's apply these ideas to our groundhog friend. He has been in hibernation, sleeping out the winter's cold, deep in a world of dreams. If he awakens and sees his shadow—his projection, or in Jungian terms, all of those aspects of himself he'd prefer to avoid—then he goes back into hiding. The grand awakening that is springtime remains far off. However, he will only see his shadow if the sun is shining brightly and he has to look away because it's too much for his sleepy eyes. Nor does he understand that the shadow he sees is of his own making. It frightens him so much that he retreats back into the safety of his burrow to lose himself again in dreaming.

If the groundhog is to remain aboveground, he needs a more gradual awakening without the shock of sunlight and scary shadows. He gets this on a cloudy day. Spared from both sun and shadow, he rests comfortably aboveground, and springtime is that much closer.

For those who stumble out of bed in the morning, heads still choked with sleep, the act of flinging open the shutters to bright daylight is hardly welcome. Not before that first cup of coffee! They need time to acclimate. The same is true for spiritual awakening. Many a spiritual seeker craves an experience of full awakening to God, or what the Course calls "revelation." Yet unless the timing is right, such an experience will prove overwhelming and potentially terrifying.*

There is no profit in fear. The Course tells us that the Holy Spirit will never lead us to any experience that's fearful, even if that's an experience of God. To the extent

---

* This is the dilemma of the Hebrew people at the base of Mount Sinai in Exodus, as I point out in *From Plagues to Miracles*. They are unprepared for a reunion with God and therefore perceive Him as terrifying.

that we still fear Him, we will not be able to reach Him. You cannot find God through fear any more than you can discover love through attack, order through chaos, or silence through noise. The "God-fearing" supplicant will remain far distant from the object of his or her worship. The Course reassures us with typically understated humor, *"Fear not that you will be abruptly lifted up and hurled into reality,"*[5] because that would be counterproductive indeed!

Along similar lines, few of us are prepared to confront our raw shadow face-to-face. Those disowned impulses and feelings flooding back down on us at once could prove shattering. Like the groundhog, we'd retreat and seek refuge in the false comfort of sleep and dreams. Our projected shadow elements have to be doled out to us at a pace that matches our preparation and readiness.

Optimum spiritual growth requires this balance of light and shadow. A gradual learning curve is the most effective, with enough light to see, but not so much that we become frightened and retreat. This is why we leave all things to the Holy Spirit. The Holy Spirit is the only one who knows your level of readiness and can guide you to the right lesson at the right time without provoking fear. He shows you how to take back your disowned projections—the obstacles you've erected to the awareness of love—and safely bring them into the light, where they dissolve back into nothingness like the shadows they are. Entrust your spiritual path to Him and Him alone. He will lead you forward at a pace that's perfect for you, custom-designed to skirt your shadows and bring you joyously into the light.

The Mirror of Self

You cannot see your own face. No one can. Think about that for a moment. It's a simple yet profound insight, which demonstrates the limits of both the body's perception and the ego. You cannot see your own face, the marker of your identity, You can only see its reflection or its representation in a photograph. You do not know yourself except indirectly.

If you want to clean up your appearance, you'll need a mirror. Otherwise you could be mussing up your hair, mis-applying makeup, and generally making a mess of yourself. With a mirror, you can at least see the things that are out of place and try to correct them. You may look better or worse than you imagined, but at least you'll know where to focus your efforts.

Because projection is so essential to how the ego works, our brothers and sisters become mirrors in which we glimpse the blemishes of our false self-concept. We see in them our own disowned shame, guilt, and fear. We can't see these in ourselves or for ourselves. We cannot see the face we present to the world.

"You will learn what you are from what you have projected onto others, and therefore believe they are."[6] Therefore, if we want metaphorically to clean up our image, we start by observing what we've projected onto others. We identify and reclaim as our own the distorted shadows we cast upon them, keeping us from truly knowing them.

How do we take back our projections and free ourselves from these shadows? We must be willing to take an honest look at our grievances. We look in the mirror they hold up to us and unflinchingly ask ourselves these questions:

- Would I accuse myself of what I am holding against the other person?
- How would I feel if I learned that someone else felt this way about me?
- Do I want to keep this grievance, knowing that if I do, I will never truly see the other person or myself?
- Or do I want to be free of this grievance in order to see them truly and through them come to know my Self?

Forgiveness is the process by which we free ourselves from projections. We take a hard look in the mirror in order to identify and remove the imagined blemishes to the face of Christ—our true face, the one we all share. We forgive the things that trigger us, recognizing that they're nothing but reflected images in the ego's hall of mirrors. By lifting the burden of our projected "sins" from them and seeing them anew in the light of holiness, we come to recognize our own holiness. We understand at last that forgiveness was never really about them or for them alone. It was always about our self and the Self we share. "*Your brother is the mirror in which you see the image of yourself as long as long as perception lasts. And perception will last until the Sonship knows itself as whole.*"[7] We never really forgive anyone else, because in truth there *is* no one else; they are one with us. Forgiveness is for us, freeing us from our own self-imposed prison.

> *It is impossible to forgive another, for it is only your sins you see in him. You want to see them there, and not in you. That is why forgiveness of another is an illusion. Yet it is the only happy dream in all the world. . . . Only in someone else can you forgive yourself.*[8]

Forgiveness is our way home, the path back to oneness. It is how we reunite the fractured pieces of the Son of God and complete the task of *tikkun olam*. It is the way we remember our Identity.

At the outset, our vision is dim, and we believe that forgiveness applies only to certain of our relationships. We may focus on our most glaring and obvious grievances—those that cause us the most pain or that seem to turn up in our lives repeatedly in relationship after relationship. Or we may prefer to forgive only the grievances that affect us so minimally that we can dispatch them with ease. In the first case, we've assigned ourselves a very heavy lift. It might prove too hard, leaving us to conclude that forgiveness is not really possible, so why bother? In the second case, we might congratulate ourselves on how well we're able to forgive while conveniently overlooking the relationships that truly challenge us. The ego can coopt anything, even the idea of forgiveness, for its purposes.

Here's the thing: you have to start somewhere, so whichever relationship catches your attention is fine—as long as you consciously partner with the Holy Spirit. You will be given plenty of opportunities to practice, but He will lead you only to those for which you're ready. And He will help you get ready for those that require the heavy lifting so that when you finally tackle them, you'll find they're no harder than any of the others.

Forgiveness begins wherever you find yourself, with those already in your life. Look around you: that's where you start. The neighbor with the barking dog, the coworker who sucks up to the boss, the friend who never calls you back, and most of all, your family—the ones you live with; the ones who leave their dirty socks on the floor, who buy things they don't need, the ones whose slightest frown or shrug of dismissal can bring you to an instant boil.

However, forgiveness is not limited to people you know personally. By practicing it, you learn to see as the Holy Spirit sees, and from His perspective, every fleeting relationship offers an opportunity for forgiveness. The passerby at whom you smiled and said hi but who failed to smile back. The guy in the fancy car who cut you off. The politician who lies all the time. Walk down any city street, drive any stretch of freeway, read your social media news feed, watch the nightly news on TV—you will be given abundant chances to practice forgiveness.

Regard forgiveness as you would your windshield wipers and washer fluid on a dark night's drive through the countryside. Your headlights illuminate the road ahead, but they also attract bugs that smash against your windshield, leaving it sullied and making it difficult to see. Like wipers and washer fluid, forgiveness must constantly sweep across the field of your vision, clearing it of the ego's debris: the judgments and grievances that splatter against your mind as you try to make your way home.

*   *   *

When we come from ego, we cannot look at *any* of our brothers or sisters without making judgments about them: their appearance, their personality, their status in the world, whether we like them and how much. Each judgment contains the seeds of specialness, grievance, or both. These judgments are so automatic and constant that once you begin to take notice of them, you feel overwhelmed. How can you possibly forgive them all? You'd be pausing every minute to call on the Holy Spirit.

There is another way to approach this. Every encounter we have with another person holds a mirror to our own face, giving us another chance to look upon the shadows we cast on others and forgive them.

> *When you meet anyone, remember it is a holy encounter. As you see him you will see yourself. As you treat him, you will treat yourself. As you think of him you will think of yourself. Never forget this, for in him you will find yourself or lose yourself.* [9]

Understand this passage, and you will understand why Jesus in the Gospels instructed you to love your neighbor as yourself. The truth is, you can *only* love your neighbor as you love yourself, and you can only love yourself to the extent that you love your neighbor. You and your neighbor are one in the eyes of the Holy Spirit. You *are* love, both of you. If you see them as anything less, or treat them as separate, different, or special, that judgment will be reflected back onto you as well. Your neighbor—which of course includes everyone everywhere—is nothing less than the mirror of self. Behold in them what you would want to see reflected in you. Do you prefer grievances? Or a vision of holiness and love? Whichever you choose is what you will see.

> *The way to recognize your brother is by recognizing the Holy Spirit in him. . . . See him through the Holy Spirit in his mind, and you will recognize Him in yours. What you acknowledge in your brother you are acknowledging in yourself, and what you share you strengthen.*[10]

DID Revisited

We saw in chapter 9 how DID can serve as a model for understanding the fracture of oneness and the separation from God, as well as what's needed to restore those fragments to their original wholeness. You'll recall that in DID, severe repetitive abuse in early childhood cleaves the mind into separate personalities or identities, each of which believes itself to be unique and distinct even though they all share the same physical body. Each alter personality sees itself as having its own body, which may differ from the actual body in age, gender, hair or eye color, abilities, or health. The alters have different personality characteristics as well—friendly, meek, domineering, belligerent, aloof, seductive—and they rarely get along or even interact with each other. These alters can emerge to take control of the physical body and behave in ways that are very uncharacteristic of the host. A prudish woman may have a seductive alter who sleeps around; a scrupulous churchgoer may harbor a thief. When an alter emerges and takes over the body, the host personality loses memory. It can reawaken into consciousness abruptly with no idea of where it is or how it got there, and dressed in clothing it doesn't recognize.

Psychotherapists who treat DID can be tempted to play favorites and take sides among the alters. Some are approachable, while others are hostile and distant. Of course you want to help the sweet scared child; of course you want to evict the abusive alter who threatens to kill that child if she keeps talking to you. But this would be a mistake. The goal of treatment is integration: helping *all* of the alters to accept each other, to recognize their interconnectedness, and ultimately to join together in a wholeness that is far more than the sum of its parts.

To accomplish this task, no alter can be left out. The tough skinhead who skips your appointments is as vital to the process as the wounded child who craves your love and attention. The therapist must be able to see the hidden value in each and hold them all in equal esteem if treatment is to be successful. In a word, she must be capable of loving every alter. She must hold in her mind the knowledge of their unity despite their apparent differences. She must also help the patient to identify the different alters and help them all to appreciate each other and the contribution each makes to the whole. In this way, the dissociative barriers that kept them separate begin to grow porous. Eventually, certain alters discover love for each other. Others follow suit. With time all come to this realization. When nothing but love remains, nothing to keep them divided and separate, it is a small, easy step for them to join and integrate as one whole mind.

In my psychotherapy with DID, I have witnessed this process play out a number of times, and it always brings me to tears. There were child alters that screamed at each other because none was getting what they needed, yet each feared the others might be favored. As each brought forth the pain they had sequestered within, revealing it to the others, they grew closer. They began to recognize their commonality and understand that none could gain at the expense of any other. They had to join in purpose if any of them were to find peace. In a word, they had to learn to forgive each other and the past they shared. The end result? They would sit together in a circle (in the patient's mind, of course) and merge into what they described afterwards as a warm, brilliant sphere of love. This experience was so intense for them, so all-encompassing, that twenty minutes could easily pass in silence until I had to gently rouse them to end our session.

One of the most powerful examples of forgiveness I have ever witnessed occurred between two alters in a woman I treated for many years, who made a number of serious suicide attempts over the course of our therapy. This woman had experienced childhood abuse so horrific that I refuse to describe it in these pages. One of the perpetrators was a physician. He had given her sedative injections prior to abusing her in order to keep her quiet and compliant. She had an alter modeled on this man. (Yes, my patient was female, but the alter was male.) Throughout the therapy he remained cold and clinically distant, as I'm sure the perpetrator had been in real life. He made it very clear that he did not approve of what I was doing. As much as I tried to engage him, he rarely joined in except with a dismissive word or two.

One day, years into treatment, he stepped forward on his own. He was distraught—in tears—which of course was a complete reversal of his demeanor up to that point. I asked him what had happened. He had momentarily decided to let down the dissociative barriers that had kept him isolated from the child alter he'd abused. In that brief instant he experienced all of her terror and pain. He kept repeating that he didn't realize how bad it was; he'd had no idea. In truth, he hadn't *wanted* to know. The dissociative barriers that kept them apart were necessary to prevent him from feeling the child's flood of emotion, which he now found too much to bear. And yet, having suspended those barriers just once, he was transformed. He would never be the same again. He could no longer hold himself aloof to inflict torture on the other alters. With this shift, my patient's suicidality vanished. Over thirty years later, she remains alive and well.

*   *   *

If we use DID as a model or metaphor for our own separated condition and how to heal it, then we recognize that we are those alter personalities—all seven billion of us and counting. We get along with some people and battle it out with others. We communicate, but only to a limited extent, because we hold back our most private thoughts, where our personal shame and grievances are sequestered. In God's reality, of course, we are one. We are dream fragments of the fractured Son of God.

If we are to awaken from our fractured dream state and rejoin as one, then, like the alters of DID, we must learn to loosen and ultimately do away with the barriers that seem to separate us. But we need help. We need a really good therapist. And who among us is in a position to play such a role? Who is able to meet us at the level of our differences yet simultaneously hold the truth of our wholeness and lead us to it?

The Holy Spirit is the ideal therapist. Indeed the Course tells us, "*The Holy Spirit is the only Therapist*."[11] He meets us where we are as dissociated alters and leads us gently toward integration. He stands at the end of time, in eternity. Therefore He knows the big picture; He knows how the story ends and that the ending is happy. Overlooking the differences that seem to separate us, He sees in each of us the holographic entirety of the Sonship. He lends us His perspective so that we too can overlook those differences and learn to forgive.

This is easier in theory than in practice. As we've noted, the differences between us seem very real, glaring, and insurmountable. How can we possibly overlook them? How can we learn to see our sisters and brothers as the Holy Spirit sees them, with Christ's vision?

Love's Litmus Test

A Course in Miracles gives us a very simple framework—a litmus test of sorts—that we can apply to every person we encounter in order to see them as the Holy Spirit does, through the lens of forgiveness. Here's how it works.

Is the other person offering you love? Is that what they're expressing? If so, then all is well, and you want to respond in kind with love. Love meets itself and extends. Or are they expressing something other than love—like anger, attack, fear, shame, or jealousy? If that is what they are offering, how do you respond then? The temptation is to return the favor and respond in kind. That's certainly the ego's way: an eye for an eye. But if they're expressing anything other than love, then obviously they must be feeling deprived of love. They feel *at-lack*. In which case, the only fitting response is to give them what they believe they're lacking: love. Either way, no matter what they bring to you, you respond with love.

> *Every loving thought is true. Everything else is an appeal for healing and help, regardless of the form it takes.*[12]

> *Only appreciation is an appropriate response to your brother. Gratitude is due him for both his loving thoughts and his appeals for help, for both are capable of bringing love into your awareness if you perceive them truly.*[13]

To respond with love does not necessarily mean that you rush to embrace them or gush over with warmth and praise. Usually a simple thought will do. The simple fact of your willingness to love is powerful in itself and can bring changes to the situation. Should you feel some action is called for, then please run an internal check with the Holy Spirit first. Follow His guidance, always. Remember, you're just an alter personality; He is the Therapist.

By applying this litmus test to our fellow alter personalities, we learn to overlook their apparent differences in favor of our commonality. We all feel lacking, and we all want love. We can bear witness to their negative attitudes without getting pulled into our own unforgiving judgments. We can actually feel appreciation for them, because their lack of love has given us an opportunity to strengthen our awareness of love's presence within ourselves. How? By sharing it. And that is forgiveness.

Love calls to love and answers as itself. We share it freely and easily, with no fear of losing it by giving it away. It brings more to both giver and receiver. Respond to your sisters and brothers with love in every circumstance, and you fulfill the commandment to love your neighbor as yourself at the deepest level of understanding.

You *are* love; they *are* love; the Self you share together is love. In Christ's vision, the vision of the Holy Spirit, there is only love, so how else could you respond to your neighbor? Love sees love, welcomes it, embraces it, and joins with it.

The Course instructs us, "*Teach only love, for that is what you are.*"[14] You cannot lose what you are. And when your neighbors—your fellow alters—awaken at last to the truth that they too are love, no matter what they had believed themselves to be, then forgiveness is complete. The joining of minds as one, united in love, becomes not only possible but inevitable and immediate.

15

Applied Forgiveness

In the previous chapter we saw that if you want to forgive, it is essential to recognize your brothers and sisters as part of your greater self. By taking back what you projected onto them and aligning your vision with the Holy Spirit's, they become accurate reflections of your true Self.

In this chapter, I would like to offer some practical tools for arriving at this insight and applying it consistently. These are not formal practices. They are new perspectives—reframes really—that allow us to see others in a different light. Think of them as corrective lenses that you can apply to your own faulty vision to bring it into alignment with the Holy Spirit's. Let's try some of these forgiveness lenses on to discover which ones might work best for you.

The Psychotherapist's Perspective

I was a psychotherapist in private practice for over thirty years before I was guided to take on a leadership role with the Foundation for Inner Peace, the publisher of *A Course in Miracles*. As such, I've worked intensively with many hundreds of people. Every time I'd walk out to my waiting room to greet a new patient for the first time, there was an element of the unknown. Whom would I meet? What would they look like? What was their mood, their body language? I was curious, because this was someone who could become part of my life for many years.

Every so often I'd meet someone whom I judged negatively. Although I didn't really know them yet, something about them sparked an immediate dislike. Had I met any of these people socially at a party or some community function, I'd be pleasant and polite but make no effort to get to know them better. There would be no opportunity to correct my snap judgments. Meeting them in my office, however, was a different story. I considered that sacred space. Such judgments had no place there. Furthermore, as a longstanding Course student, I believed that everyone who sought my help had something to teach me as well. Each offered the potential for a holy encounter. So how did I handle my own negative judgments?

Over the years I adopted the practice of mentally reciting before each session a particular prayer from *A Course in Miracles*. It's commonly referred to as the Prayer for Salvation, and it came to Bill Thetford in response to a direct need of his. Early in the scribing of the Text, Bill was invited to attend a conference on juvenile diabetes. He was a psychologist, not an MD, and therefore knew nothing about diabetes. Nonetheless, he felt compelled to go for reasons involving departmental politics. Because of his ignorance about the topic, he felt extremely anxious. What if someone asked him a question about diabetes? He'd have no idea how to answer. And so he asked Helen for some guidance from the Voice that dictated the Course. In response she received the following prayer, which he was to recite to himself whenever his anxiety arose.

> *I am here only to be truly helpful.*
> *I am here to represent Him Who sent me.*
> *I do not have to worry about what to say or what to do,*
> *   because He Who sent me will direct me.*
> *I am content to be wherever He wishes, knowing He goes*
> *   there with me.*
> *I will be healed, as I let Him teach me to heal.*[1]

These words helped Bill immensely, as they have done for many Course students over the years. We speak this prayer aloud at the start of every important meeting of the Foundation for Inner Peace to affirm our goal and our need for guidance. Its words remind us that there is no need to plan—in fact, all planning comes from the ego, and no matter the apparent outcome, it will always get in the way of the Holy Spirit's agenda. All that's asked of us is to show up wherever we're guided. We are ambassadors for the Holy Spirit and His message of love. If we adopt the proper mind-set right up front, it doesn't matter where in the dream we happen to find ourselves or whom we happen to be with. We will receive the words and actions most helpful to the situation and everyone it touches.

With this in mind, I would silently dedicate each psychotherapy session to the goal of being "truly helpful" in order "to represent Him Who sent me"; to trust that I was in the right place at the right time with the right person, and that my words would be guided; and to invoke the goal of healing, not only for my patient, but for myself as well. As we saw in the last chapter, if we are all reflections of each other, then it is impossible for me to help them without also receiving the help they bring to me. Their healing *is* mine and mine *is* theirs. We walk side by side on the path to wholeness.

The words of this prayer are not a magical incantation. They are a concise and straightforward statement of Course principles. They will be useful only to the extent that you choose to follow them and let them guide you. For me, in my psychotherapy practice, they provided a way of focusing my intent to help. But without my willingness, they would be just so many empty words.

What does it mean to be "truly helpful" in the context of psychotherapy? It means that I acknowledge what I don't know and cannot know, because such knowing is beyond my ability. I also acknowledge that I am not in charge of the healing process. As a result, I don't try to figure out how to help my patient based solely on my clinical training and past experience. I forgo judgment. Instead I step back and allow myself to become as clear a channel as possible for wisdom greater than my own to come forth. In that context, my training and experience can be put to good use under the direction of the Holy Spirit. He is in charge, not me. He understands my patient's problems and their real needs far better than I ever will.

What about those snap judgments I made about certain patients? When I am being "truly helpful," they quickly prove irrelevant. Whatever I as an ego might think of someone doesn't matter. The simple fact that they've shown up in my office asking for help is all that counts. They are my brother or sister, and our mutual goal is peace. They are calling out for love. As the Holy Spirit's emissary, that is what I can bring. Through Him I learn to love them as my Self.

One of my greatest challenges in this regard was a veteran of one of America's many wars, a man who came to me racked with terrible guilt over the deaths of his fellow GIs. He was very likable, and I felt compassion for him immediately. But he was a voracious consumer of right-wing talk radio, listening for hours every day, and he sure hated those liberals—a label that accurately described my own political leanings. Even more challenging was the fact that he had poor hygiene. He stank of sweat and urine. Following each of our sessions I had to spray and wipe down the leather couch on which he sat, trying to eradicate as best I could his strong odor in hopes that my next patient wouldn't notice.

The part of our brain that registers smell is very old and primitive. It sits right in front of, and is wired directly into, the midbrain limbic system which is the source of our emotions. As a result, we tend to react with particularly strong feelings to anything or anyone that smells bad. No doubt this once served a survival function, but it also became a rationale for bias and prejudice. Those who smell bad—who don't smell "like us"—are judged as inferior and rejected. The cold sneer of contempt with the upper lip retracted is actually the same facial gesture we make in response to a noxious odor.* It has morphed from its original meaning to become an expression of condemnation.

My patient's odor posed a real problem for me. Because if my office was truly sacred space, then it shouldn't reek of urine and sweat! What would my other patients think?

At the same time, I also sensed that if I raised the issue and asked this man to clean up before our sessions, he would feel ashamed, and I would lose his trust. I would be handing him a good excuse to quit therapy in order to avoid dealing with his painful psychological wounds, as he had for most of his life. The purpose of our relationship would go unfulfilled. So I chose to say nothing.

As the therapy progressed, we relived together the horrors he'd experienced on the battlefield. I sat with him as he wept in despair over fallen comrades and then later laughed with relief as his guilt lifted. And a strange thing occurred. I found that I no longer resented the chore of cleaning up after him. If this was part of the service I was called upon to perform for my brother, so be it. His strong fragrance would not get in the way of the healing work we had com-

---

* This insight comes from the work of Silvan Tomkins, PhD, the mentor of Donald Nathanson, MD, who was mentioned in chapter 5 with regard to the topic of shame.

mitted to doing together. Indeed, he made unusually rapid progress—for which we both felt grateful—and we were able to complete our work in a matter of mere months.

I share this story because I think that the relationship between doctor and patient in psychotherapy offers a good model for how to practice forgiveness in *any* relationship. The ego struts forward and rudely thrusts its judgments in our face. We can accept these and use them as grounds for a grievance *or* we can remember that we have a higher goal, an overarching purpose that includes everyone. In any relationship, both parties want peace. Both want love. As in psychotherapy, one of us might be more aware of this desire than the other and more practiced in bringing it about, but that's just fine. Our greater awareness will serve us by helping us recognize the call for love in someone we might otherwise have judged and to provide what is lacking: love. Whether or not the other person responds in kind is not the point. *We* will feel better, and we can trust that in the fullness of time so will they.

*   *   *

Shortly after completing the final edit of the Course proper, Helen Schucman scribed the first of two supplements to *A Course in Miracles:* a twenty-three page pamphlet titled *Psychotherapy: Purpose, Process, and Practice.* (This is now included in the combined third edition of *A Course in Miracles* published by the Foundation for Inner Peace.) Although addressed to psychotherapists, it is a succinct yet comprehensive summation of Course principles and therefore applicable to everyone. One of its central points is that *all healing, of both mind and body, is fundamentally psycho-therapy.* This is so because the separated ego-mind is the source of all illness, and only the mind can reverse what it has brought about and allow healing to occur. As the Course sees it, there is no difference between healing and forgiveness. You cannot heal without forgiving, and if you truly forgive, healing will follow naturally. In this sense, we are all psychotherapists. As the Psychotherapy supplement states, *"Everyone is both patient and therapist in every rela-tionship in which he enters."*[2] We are all engaged in healing the fractured Son of God. We are tasked with fulfilling the sacred goal of *tikkun olam.*

As you go about your day, moving in and out of rela-tionships that involve many different forms and degrees of intimacy, think of yourself as a psychotherapist working in tandem with the Holy Spirit. You have a sacred duty to heal. Yes, there may be things about the other person that you'll judge and disapprove of. None of them are important if your only goal is to be "truly helpful." It is *your* respon-sibility to maintain this perspective in order to facilitate healing for yourself and for your fellow "patients" trapped here alongside you in the ego's nightmare asylum.

The Twins Perspective

Every good screenwriter understands that conflict is essen-tial for a good story. Without conflict, we rapidly grow bored. Conflict is generated by differences, whether that's two personalities who clash, opposing goals that get in the way of each other, or mutually exclusive plans for how to reach those goals. The story shapes itself around the conflict and our efforts to deal with it.

The ego, of course, is all about conflict, and this is reflected in the life story of every human being, whether actual or fictional. In fiction, the hero usually comes up with some kind of satisfying resolution, at which point the end credits roll across the screen, and you get up and go home. Story over. In life there are no such artificial end points. We seem to move from one struggle to the next. There is always another battle to fight, another hill to climb, until at last one of them kills us. This may make for an exciting movie, but it's a lousy script for achieving peace.

What if there were no conflict in your world? What if there were no differences from which conflict could arise, or at least none of any consequence? Without differences, there could be no judgments and no conflict. How might this be possible?

Imagine that you were born into a world populated entirely by identical twins? Everyone you met, everyone you knew—all identical. Each an exact replica of you. You inhabit a world populated by reflections of yourself. Now take this a step further. Each twin has had the same upbringing as you and experienced the same series of events throughout life. Each knows precisely what you and all the others have gone through. There are no surprises and no separate life stories, because all are one and the same.

Pretty dull, you say. Perhaps. But what exactly is it you're missing? Contrast? Variety? Challenge? Call it by any name you like, it is not an experience of peace, and therefore it can only be conflict in one form or another. Once you recognize this, you can ask yourself: *is conflict what I really want*? A part of you actually does, and we know its name and how it got there. But the ego's goals are not yours. If you seek conflict, you cannot simultaneously seek peace. You can't step left and right, or backward and forward, at the same time. Try it, and you wind up standing still. It is not possible to serve two masters. Your goal is either conflict or peace, one or the other.

To return to our world of twins, isn't this exactly how we appear to the Holy Spirit? He doesn't credit our differences: the myriad variations among bodies and their tales of triumph and woe. He sees only what is true in us, unchanging and unchangeable. He sees spirit. At the level of spirit, we *are* the same. We are identical twins—a set of septabillion-tuplets—all carrying the "genetic" imprint of love from our shared Source: God.

In order to forgive, you must learn to overlook superficial differences and realize that they are superficial. This is not easy, because, in typical ego fashion, you register those differences as real and *then* try to banish them from your mind. But what if you started from a different premise? What if you already understood that everyone is your twin? Then it becomes easier. You naturally look past their differences, because you know that, as spirit, they're identical to you.

It's as if you were born wearing a thick pair of glasses that distorted your vision, forcing you to see everyone as different, and now the Holy Spirit lifts them gently from your eyes and frees you to behold them as they really are. Those differences you once perceived? Gone. It turns out they were never real, just distortions introduced by the ego. All that remains is spirit, which is the same in everyone.

As you go through your day, you might also think of it this way. You are participating in a grand masquerade, whirling and dancing about in an infinitely large ballroom thronged with countless revelers, all of whom have disguised themselves by wearing elaborate masks and all varieties of clothing. They appear to be strikingly different—captivating or disgusting, inviting or threatening—but the differences you see are simply part of the masquerade. Behind the masks lies sameness. You *know* this. You are not fooled by such apparent differences. When at last the music stops and it's time to go home, everyone flips up their mask and you gaze upon their true face. What you see is your own face, the face of spirit—nothing more, nothing less. They are your twins, descended from the same lineage, and you love them as your Self.

The Reincarnation Perspective

The concept of reincarnation plays no role in the Course's teachings. Although it does address the topic in the Manual for Teachers and there are a few infrequent lines suggestive of reincarnation, it neither endorses nor criticizes those who choose to believe in past lives. It does make the point that, in the ultimate sense, reincarnation cannot be real—but then neither is the life you think you're living now. If time and the body are both illusions, what does it matter whether you've lived one life or a thousand? They're all part of the same dream—the ego's dream of separation.

Like everything in the ego's world, reincarnation has value only if it is used to support the goal of awakening. To the extent that it moves you in the direction of this goal, it is helpful. Otherwise—if you use it to bolster your own sense of specialness ("I was Cleopatra; you were Mark Antony")—it becomes just another ego-imposed obstacle to awakening.

The world contains multitudes of different people. If you live only one lifetime, then you're stuck in your fixed perception. If you are poor and the man on the hill is rich, you must live with that inequity and your feelings about it. You are who you are; they are who they are. Not much room for change. If you feel undying hatred for him, well, that's just the way it is. There's no getting around it, because you're both locked into your particular identities.

On the other hand, if everyone has lived numerous lifetimes and will live many more, how can you be certain that the person who most irritates you wasn't your precious child in some prior lifetime? You can't. Your vision is confined to their outer form as it appears in this one lifetime. The idea of reincarnation becomes a helpful lens for looking beyond the other person's current appearance and behavior to see them across time as someone you're more able to love.

If you knew with absolute certainty that your nutty supervisor—the one who demands the impossible and criticizes you mercilessly—had been your brother in a past life and had gladly sacrificed himself so that you could survive, mightn't that change how you feel about him? If the uncle who abused you had been the victim of *your* abuse in some past life, wouldn't you be in a better position to release the hurt? And if your difficult child was destined to become your parent in the next go-round, might you be kinder and more understanding?

The corrective lens of reincarnation can be applied broadly for the purpose of forgiveness because in the fullness of time *anyone* could have been, or could become, anyone else: your trusted parent, your cherished child, your beloved partner. By viewing them in this way, you superimpose a different form over the one you currently see, a form that frees you to be more loving. It's a reframe of sorts. In place of a threatening adversary, you look upon someone you once treasured or will love in your next lifetime.

Remember, outer appearances are unreal. The ego's world spins off countless different forms, all of which are changing, none of which will endure. This includes the bodily forms we take on in reincarnation. Bodies don't matter. The form doesn't matter. What matters is *content*, namely, the love behind the form. Therefore, if you choose to perform a mental makeover and transform someone you dislike into someone you're capable of loving, reincarnation becomes a useful conceptual tool.

The forgiving lens of reincarnation can also be applied to historical figures and those in the news you harbor grievances against. If all outer appearances are equally unreal, over the course of time anyone could become someone very different.

Let's return to Hitler. Seen through reincarnation's lens, he too will cycle through many different lifetimes, each with its own lessons. But the ultimate outcome of his journey is foreordained. He will return to love, because that's his reality too. Even if he's the last being in the universe to finally get it and awaken, in the end he must. It's already happened! And what might the being who was Hitler look like in its final lifetime, the one in which enlightenment is finally achieved? Who will Hitler be then? What loving acts will he perform? Knowing this is his destiny, could you now consider forgiving him?

According to the Course, time is a "*vast illusion in which figures come and go*."³ Its purpose, in the hands of the Holy Spirit, is to "give us time" to learn the lessons of forgiveness at our own ideal pace. So how can we judge someone for their behavior at any given point in time? I have two nephews, both now young adults, both decent, caring human beings, but as children they were terrors. Do I judge them for who they were, or for who they've become? Which of those two judgments is more accurate? Which aligns better with the Holy Spirit's vision? Most significantly, which frees me from *my* past and enables me to be the most loving?

There is one more way to use reincarnation in support of forgiveness. If you are not limited to a single lifetime and if all outer appearances are equally unreal, then you could have been anyone who's ever lived. Take any historical event about which you hold judgments, and recognize that all the characters in that drama are you. You were Roosevelt and Churchill, but also Hitler, Mussolini, and Stalin. You were Gandhi and Machiavelli, Abe Lincoln and Vlad the Impaler. You were a proud member of the flight crew that dropped the atomic bomb to end World War II, and you were a resident of Hiroshima staring aghast at that unholy fireball in the seconds before it consumed you and destroyed everyone you loved. You were Judas and Caiaphas; Pontius Pilate, Barabbas, Mary Magdalene, and each of the twelve disciples. And of course you were Jesus, who awakened to his true Identity as the Christ, an Identity he shared with you and continues to share. But this does not make you special, because everyone you encounter was also Jesus. Behind that mask of individuality and difference lies the face of Christ. Behind every grievance you hold against anyone, your savior stands, patient and smiling. She waits for *your* forgiveness in order to set you free.

> *We will . . . take the role assigned to us as part of God's salvation plan . . . when we allow each one we meet to save us, and refuse to hide his light behind our grievances. To everyone you meet, and to the ones you think of or remember from the past, allow the role of savior to be given, that you may share it with him.*[4]

From this perspective, each lifetime and every event within each lifetime has either taught you love and joining or grievance and separation. Each revealed to you your savior or your adversary. Each brought you closer to God or thrust you deeper into dreaming. And here you are now, reading this book, wanting to understand, learning to see your neighbor as yourself and share the love that belongs to you both.

As you near the journey's end and awaken, like Jesus, to your true Identity as the Christ, it will not matter who you were, who you are, or who you will be. It will not matter whether any particular person played the role of parent or child, victim or slayer, betrayer or beloved. The love you feel for them will be far greater than anything you have felt from any relationship of this world. They have become the living embodiment of God's love and an accurate reflection of yourself as God knows you to be. When forgiveness has brought you to this knowingness, your work here is done and God takes the final step to welcome you Home.

Forgiving through Time: New Beginnings

There is a common saying that time heals all wounds. For those bleeding out from their wounds, however, this is pretty thin solace. How long must they suffer before time at last works its magic and releases them? Nonetheless, there is wisdom here. Given time, our perspective on our wounds does indeed shift and in ways that help our grievances give way to forgiveness.

Think of someone who treated you badly when you were young and in school. Perhaps they teased or snubbed you, or goaded you into fights. Perhaps they stole your boyfriend or girlfriend. Or perhaps they were just the kind of person who soaked up all the attention in the room and left you standing unseen in their shadow. At the time this felt deeply wounding. Maybe you cried. Maybe you nursed fantasies of revenge. You may have even considered suicide. Whatever the circumstances, this person became your nemesis, and a powerful grievance was born.

As the years rolled by, this person drifted out of your life. They moved on, you moved on. You met new people. You experienced successes and a few setbacks too. You learned and grew from both. Your self-concept changed. You're not that little schoolkid anymore. Sure, you still occasionally think back on those difficult years and your old adversary, but they take up less and less of your mental space. You have better things to occupy your mind.

Then one day you run into this person, perhaps at a class reunion or social function. Now you have a choice. You can reopen those old wounds and bind that person to the image you hold of them from the past. Of course, this binds you to your old self-image as well—maybe not what you want anymore. Or you can encounter them as if you'd never met them before and shared no history together. You can view them through the lens of what Buddhists call "beginner's mind": the clear, open perception with which we greet new experiences, before judgments have a chance to form and harden. Just as you've changed, so in all likelihood have they. With beginner's mind, you can encounter them as if for the first time, free of judgment. Without the past to encumber you, you meet each other anew, *in the now.*

From this new perspective, you might find you like who this person has become. Or perhaps you pick up some new information that helps you reframe their hurtful behavior. They were cruel because they themselves were treated roughly at home. They kept you distant to hide a secret shame. Should it turn out that this person hasn't changed a bit and is still the same old jerk you remembered, you're no longer stuck with them. At the end of the event you will walk away, back to your separate lives. In each instance, your grievance has loosened its grip on you. Forgiveness become easier.

You can apply beginner's mind to any person or situation about which you've formed a judgment, negative or positive. Remember, specialness will blind you to truth fully as much as grievances. Strip away your judgments from the past, meet them in the present moment, and what do you see? Who are they *now*? Who are they *in the now*? Go further still and invite the Holy Spirit to show them to you as He sees them. Once again, you will behold the face of Christ. Your own true face.

Remember, "*the present* is *forgiveness.*"[5] Without the past there can be neither sin nor sinner. Nothing ever happened to disturb God's Son. "*What you thought your brother did to you has not occurred.*"[6]

> *Let us be still an instant, and forget all things we ever learned, all thoughts we had, and every preconception that we hold of what things mean and what their purpose is. Let us remember not our own ideas of what the world is for. We do not know. Let every image of everyone be loosened from our minds and swept away.*
>
> *Be innocent of judgment, unaware of any thoughts of evil or of good that ever crossed your mind of anyone. Now do you know him not. But you are free to learn of him, and learn of him anew. Now is he born again to you, and you are born again to him without the past that sentenced him to die, and you with him. Now is he free to live as you are free, because an ancient learning passed away, and left a place for truth to be reborn.*[7]

Forgiving through Time: Endings

Beginner's mind is one way to utilize time, or rather suspend it, in service of forgiveness. There is another and I call it *last-timer's mind*. Consider it a bookend to beginner's mind. Last-timer's mind is the perspective you gain when you've lived through a particular episode in your life so thoroughly, so completely, that you know beyond any doubt that you are done with it forever. You've squeezed from it all the lesson power it had to offer and you're ready to move on.

We can experience last-timer's mind when we arrive at any major life transition, like moving away from a familiar area, being discharged from the military, finalizing a divorce, or retiring. The feeling rarely lasts long, because we dive right into the next phase of life and quickly find ourselves embroiled in new challenges with new people. We look ahead in anticipation of the things we want to achieve rather than taking stock of where we've been.

My first experience of last-timer's mind came in the days immediately preceding my college graduation. I'd finished the last of my exams and turned in my final papers. Exhausted but exhilarated, I wandered aimlessly around campus, taking in all the familiar sights and places I'd frequented, knowing that soon I'd be leaving and would never again see them in the same way.

I came upon a good friend sprawled on the lawn, his back against a tree, a six-pack of beer by his side. He waved me over and offered me a bottle, which I gratefully accepted. We clinked our bottles in a toast and sat together grinning in silence. Not much to say. College was over.

Finished. For us both. We shook our heads in disbelief. Four years had passed in a flash. One era was ending, and a new one about to begin, but that new one would not find us together. Everything that had occurred in the span of those four years was now neatly bundled into one basket labeled "college." No further choices to be made, no use for regrets, and no point holding on to grievances, because the epoch to which they belonged was passing. We were graduating and moving on.

Like beginner's mind, last-timer's mind is incompatible with holding grievances. This is so because, if a grievance still burns inside you, then you are *not* finished; you cannot truly move on; there is still learning that remains. Any attempt to prematurely declare it finished when it still haunts you will only drive it underground and perpetuate it in your mind. You change the scenery, but the grievance remains. You're not done till you're done.

What is the hallmark of last-timer's mind? It's all about completion. When we are truly complete with a situation or relationship, we are at peace *no matter what the outcome was.* There is no further appeal in looking back to relive your triumphs and relitigate your conflicts. You were treated unfairly? Perhaps, but it's over and done. It's not worth another moment's thought. You felt demeaned, insulted, underappreciated? So be it. You're about to start a new journey. As with nineteenth-century sailors embarking on a voyage of a year or more, when that shoreline recedes into the distance and finally disappears altogether, it takes with it all your cares and woes. They're no longer relevant to the journey ahead.

The aging process can be an entry to last-timer's mind. Aging offers a wider perspective on life, a larger context within which to evaluate the impact of any given experience. With aging comes a wisdom unavailable to the young. The elderly have lived through storms and recessions; they've fallen in and out of love; they've witnessed deaths and births, prosperity and poverty, strife and peace. The calamity of the moment feels less devastating to them because of all they've seen and lived through.

From this broader perspective, it becomes harder to form grievances and easier to let them go. The school years felt toxic and suffocating when they accounted for half your life; far less so when they represent but a tiny fraction of what you've lived through. Put a drop of poison in a glass of water and toss it down—it will kill you. That same drop dispersed in the waters of a lake will have no effect, no matter how much of it you gulp down.

I remember how devastated I felt over the ending of my first marriage. At the time, it was an inconceivable loss, even though I knew it was right. Now, try as I might, I can no longer call up that feeling of hurt. It is a memory of pain, hollowed out by the years until the pain itself thins almost to nothingness.

When loss is fresh and the wound wide open, holding a grievance feels justified and natural. Your cheating spouse deserves nothing short of ruin. Buffered by decades of intervening experience, however, that grievance becomes harder to sustain. My grandmother Minnie had to work at staying hurt and angry. She needed reminders in the form of mutilated family photos. What's the point in staying furious at your cheating ex-spouse, when both of you have gone on to find new partners with whom you're much happier? Who would plunge a knife back into a wound that's finally healing?

*   *   *

Studies of near-death experiences have shown that in dying we pass through a number of different stages. The first of these is a comprehensive life review. All events from the life just lived—every decision you made along with its consequences—play out before you simultaneously. You can see very clearly where you chose well, but also where your choices led to hurt, pain, shame, and fear, for yourself and those around you. Researchers label this life review *panoramic memory*. Whereas normal memory focuses narrowly on only one incident, this is a remembering (or reliving) of the entire panorama of your life.

Often this review takes place in the presence of an all-loving being—someone like Jesus or a nonhuman entity of pure light. This presence makes no judgments about the choices you've made. The life review is not a prelude to heaven or hell. It's not about reward or punishment. It's simply an accounting: surveying the big picture in order to see how your life worked out. What lessons were learned? In what areas is there a need for more learning? Such insights often lead to a decision to return from approaching death in order to finish up incomplete life lessons.

You don't have wait to die to gain the overarching perspective of panoramic memory. You can perform a life review for the space of a single day, preferably just before going to sleep. Identify the microgrievances from the day just passed. Note any encounters where you felt a twinge of irritation, a gust of sadness, the weight of shame. Apply the Holy Spirit's litmus test of love: were there times when you chose not to be loving? Did you respond to anyone calling for love with anything other than love? All such incidents are ripe for forgiveness.

Similarly, you could do your review at the end of the week. What better use for the Sabbath? Birthdays and New Year's are also natural times to look back, take stock, and make corrections in order to move forward unencumbered by the past.

Parting in Forgiveness

You've lived your entire life in a small mountain village. The village sits in the crook of a valley nestled between several high peaks. You've grown up there, learned the ways of village life, begun relationships, and ended them. You've worked for and alongside the village elders. Some you respected and learned from; others you merely tolerated. But now a powerful urge has bloomed within you, and you know that the time has come to say farewell to your village and move on.

You murmur a few quiet goodbyes. You share heartfelt hugs. And you set out, climbing the steep, winding path that threads its way up the mountainside. As you climb, the village below grows smaller and smaller. There it is—the place where you've lived your entire life. You'd thought it was the whole world; now it could fit in the palm of your hand. Its houses and shops, streets and towers—all are dwarfed by the surrounding peaks.

As you near the crest of the mountain, you look back at the tiny village, taking it all in, recalling with bittersweet fondness everything that took place there. It all worked to bring you to this point. Where you're headed, it's of no more consequence.

You silently bless it all. Then you turn and cross over the crest of the ridge. An entirely new vista opens before you. Your village is no more, as if it had never existed. The new awaits, beckoning, calling you forward. You begin your descent, step by step, unhurried, fully ready and welcoming whatever may come. Last-timer's mind becomes beginner's mind.

16

Intimacy: The Forgiveness Challenge

We said earlier that relationships are the classrooms in which the Holy Spirit schools us in His curriculum of love. Through relationships, we learn the truth of what we are and recognize that same truth shining from our brothers and sisters. Relationships demonstrate the many maneuvers we use to block love's presence and also show how to remove those blocks. Through our relationships, we learn what has value and what has none. This learning goes by many different names in *A Course in Miracles*—Atonement, salvation, healing, forgiveness, vision—but all describe the same fundamental process: letting go of the ego's illusions in order to experience truth, love, and wholeness.

Levels of Learning

The Course, in its Manual for Teachers, describes three levels of relationship within which teaching and learning take place. (These levels have meaning only within the ego's world, where orders of magnitude appear to be real.) The first level involves casual encounters, such as the one with the boys on the elevator from chapter 11. Here the opportunities for learning are specific and highly circumscribed. They are also fairly obvious, and they tend not to affect us for very long. The second level involves a more sustained relationship, in which two people come together for a more prolonged period of time and then go their separate ways. This would include certain friendships, workplace colleagues, and romantic pairings that didn't work out. The third level applies to relationships that are lifelong. *"These are teaching-learning situations in which each person is given a chosen learning partner who presents him with unlimited opportunities for learning."*[1] They generally consist of parents, children, and life partners, although occasionally other long-term relationships would qualify (such as Helen Schucman's and Bill Thetford's). They are not necessarily positive, nor are they easy. They give us an opportunity to apply the Holy Spirit's litmus test on a consistent, ongoing basis and "teach only love" no matter what comes our way. Although every relationship at every level holds out the possibility of forgiving and healing, it is in these long-term, level-three relationships that we do the heavy lifting of forgiveness. You might think of them as your master class.

Intimate Strangers?

When we try to imagine what it would be like to practice unconditional love—love without judgments, preferences, or limits—we might imagine ourselves turning the other cheek and loving our enemies. Or we might picture ourselves wandering the world in long white robes, beaming beatific smiles of perfect love to every passing stranger. Ironically, these portrayals tend to leave out our most intimate everyday relationships. After all, these are the people we already love, or want to love, or try our best to love. They're our inner circle, so how can they be the problem? Yet in my experience, it's often easier to love a stranger precisely because *you don't know them*. You're *not* intimate. You haven't had to deal with their flaws, their bad habits, the unsavory things they may have done in the past. It's easier to blanket strangers with love and forgiveness, because it's abstract. You don't know them, so there's nothing much to judge.

This was brought home to me in 1980 during my junior year of medical school, when I decided to take the intensive EST training developed by Werner Erhard. It took place over two consecutive weekends. I recall entering a large conference hall jammed with people and taking a seat in between two random strangers. Our charismatic trainer thrilled us with clever arguments designed to lead us to powerful, life-changing insights. In the process, we did a number of exercises that required us to share intimate details of our lives with those sitting next to us.

Sharing painful, personal memories and feelings with a stranger? Seriously? How awkward! How intrusive! I could feel the room tensing with anticipatory resistance, including my own. But after a round or two of this sharing, an interesting thing happened. I got used to it. My neighbors were in the same awkward position, after all, and we learned to laugh together at our stories and grow teary over our missteps and failings. The sharing brought us closer . . . sort of. In a limited way. Because whatever degree of intimacy we developed, at the end of the weekend we parted ways and returned home to our separate lives. When the training wrapped up, we said goodbye knowing we would probably never meet again. The things we shared provoked some important insights, and there's no doubt that exposing them in this relatively safe setting helped to release some shame. There were moments of real unconditional love too. But for me it all had very little traction, because the relationships were not *truly* intimate. They were level-one relationships repackaged to feel like level three.

At the conclusion of the two weekends, I stood in line to say thank-you to our trainer, whom by this point I esteemed as an engaging and brilliant human being only a step shy of full enlightenment. I looked him in the eye and expressed my sincere thanks. I embraced him in a big hug. Much to my surprise, he did not reciprocate. His hug was tentative—not quite standoffish, but stiff and awkward. This man who on stage came off as warm, loving, and genuine was apparently incapable of giving a decent hug. He was only an actor skilled at seducing his audience into a facsimile of intimacy, which was unsustainable when faced with the intimacy of a genuine hug.

During this same period, knowing that I was headed for a career in psychiatry, I signed up for a nine-month group-therapy experience. Eight young adults from all walks of life gathered weekly in a small, unadorned room to share our innermost thoughts and feelings—not so much about our lives outside the group, but about each other. Whom did we admire? Who triggered us? Who was being helpful, and who was just spouting bullshit? In retrospect, it was an incubator for identifying patterns of judgment and honestly bringing them forth in a safe setting.

The group had only met for a couple months by the time I completed the EST training, but the contrast was remarkable and instructive. Although we began the group as strangers, we grew to know each other well. We didn't always like each other. There were disagreements. People took sides. But through it all, we developed a degree of mutual respect and caring. In a word, we grew intimate.

One of the biggest factors in bringing about this intimacy was the fact that we couldn't run or hide. We had all committed to showing up for every session. If someone managed to evade a question or ignore a pointed comment in one session, they could count on the fact that it would be thrust at them again the following week. In EST, it was possible to "love 'em and leave 'em" with no consequences. In the therapy group, you couldn't get away with that.

Nevertheless, even here, in a setting devoted to safe, honest expression and helpful feedback, the intimacy we developed was limited. We formed grievances and forgave them, but we met for only ninety minutes once a week in an artificial setting stripped of the demands of ordinary life. We didn't have to contend with greasy dishes in the sink, late bills, a messy bed, or the countless minor irritations and conflicts that arise from living with someone.

At the end of nine months, the therapy group disbanded. Our relationships were time-limited: level two, not level three. The goodbye hugs we shared were full and genuine, but that only made the parting more painful. Nor could I deny that I felt relief that the group was finished. No longer would I be called upon to bare my raw emotions or forced to sit and listen to comments about myself that were painful, especially when they felt all too true. I could return to the safe anonymity of my life.

While all this was going on—EST, group therapy, medical school—I had already become a dedicated student of *A Course in Miracles*. I had studied the Text and practiced the Workbook lessons daily for over four years. I participated in a weekly study group. Inevitably I compared both my EST training and my group-therapy experience with the teachings of the Course. In that light, both were exposed as half-measures. Each offered insights that could have served as catalysts for change, but neither addressed the real source of the problem: the core beliefs and judgments that propped up my false, egoic self-concept. They approached relationships as the ego sees them, as arrangements worked out between two psychologically flawed human beings who seek love, but, fearing it, choose specialness instead.

Furthermore, although it was my choice to participate in both groups, there was a powerful implicit pressure to expose thoughts and feelings that I never would have shared in any other setting. In theory this sharing was voluntary, but in practice it was compelled. As a result, it was not truly safe, nor was it entirely genuine. My ego judged what to share, how much, and how deeply. Some of that sharing was motivated by a genuine desire for growth, but much of it was competitive: who was best at baring their soul; who had endured the most suffering; who was wisest, kindest, most experienced, most likable. All too often, the sharing was used as plumage to attract a partner. *Look how open and genuine I am. How caring. And such a good listener. Let's go home together and make babies.* Sharing that's motivated by competition or seduction is counterproductive. It reinforces the ego by endorsing its goals and its need for specialness. Meanwhile, the capacity to love unconditionally as God loves remains out of reach.

The ego is incapable of undoing itself. It will resist the threat posed by love with every fiber of its pseudo-being. Sometimes that resistance will take the form of self-improvement on the theory that if you can buff and polish your self-image sufficiently, you'll have no need for God.

The Course tells us that the ego loves to analyze itself—in part to bolster its sense of self-importance and in part because it knows such analysis will go nowhere. It's another form of diversion to keep you from dealing with the real problem, which is the ego itself.

No Order of Grievances

If I were to ask which of your relationships were most in need of forgiveness, odds are you'd come up with a list of people whom you believe wronged you in some way or with whom you've had significant conflict. Maybe they insulted you, attacked you physically, or stole something precious from you, like a job or a spouse. Maybe you put your trust in them and they betrayed you.

Hollywood has made a fortune filling our minds with horrific images like that of the murder of child. We view them and tell ourselves we could never forgive such things. But most of us do not need to and never will, because what we see in the movies and on TV hasn't happened to us. We use the possibility of such calamities to make forgiveness seem like an impossible goal. As a result, the things in our lives that are in need of forgiveness go unnoticed. We give them a pass because they don't seem big enough to require forgiving.

The Course tells us that *all* things within the world of illusion are *equally* unreal and therefore *equally* in need of forgiveness. No tragedy, no grievance is worse than any other in this respect. Anything that stands in the way of love and forgiveness—even the slightest passing thought—is equally destructive of inner peace and calls us to forgive.

> *What is not love is murder. What is not loving must be an attack. Every illusion is an assault on truth, and every one does violence to the idea of love because it seems to be of equal value.*[2]

To the Holy Spirit there is no hierarchy in forms of attack. Either attack is real and you are a body, vulnerable to hurt and destined to die, or attack is unreal, an element of the ego's nightmare, and you are spirit: invulnerable and eternal. It's one way or the other; there's no compromise. "*What is not love is murder.*"

Given this, if we focus only on what we consider to be the big grievances in our lives—if we neglect those that spring up day to day and minute by minute because we judge them as trivial and not worth our attention—we are not doing the work of forgiveness. We must learn to be vigilant for *any* thought or behavior that is less than loving.

No doubt this feels like an impossible task. The ego will try to convince you that it is. It will point out all your lapses and failures—all those times when you could have and should have forgiven—until they feel so overwhelming that you conclude it is impossible and give up. Note that in the ego's judgment, grievances are either too big or too many to forgive. It never welcomes forgiveness.

As always, the ego is deceiving you. Forgiveness is like a muscle we rarely exercise. We've allowed it to atrophy to the point where we no longer remember how to use it. Like any ability, it requires practice. The more you practice, the easier it gets. Eventually forgiveness becomes your natural response to whatever judgment or grievance your mind conjures up. The freedom this brings cannot be adequately described.

Everyday Forgiveness

In the first book of this series, *From Never-Mind to Ever-Mind,* I used the term *everyday miracles* to make the point that miracles should not be viewed as extraordinary and reserved only for the really big problems. We could say the same about forgiveness.

Everyday forgiveness is the only forgiveness there is: every day and every moment of the day. It's a blanket response to grievances large and small—whatever arises. And who are the ones most likely to trigger these grievances? Whom do we live with, think about, stew over, snap at? Our level-three relationships.

For the vast majority, these level-three relationships pose the greatest challenges and offer the most opportunities to practice forgiveness. Yet somehow we do not. We make a decision, often barely conscious, *not* to deal with them, because after all they're hardly worth the trouble. If we neglect to clean them up properly and promptly, however, they pile up atop each other. They back up in the mind until, like a clogged sewer line, the accumulated grievances spill over and stink up everything.

How many older couples—couples who have lived together for thirty or more years—seem truly happy? How many greet each other with genuine hugs and smiles in the morning? How many remain polite, affectionate, and considerate to each other? All too often they're irritable and angry, snarling and snapping and arguing over the silliest of disagreements. A misplaced teacup or a five-minute delay in leaving for an appointment become grounds for character assassination. But it's not really the problem of the moment they're reacting to. It's the years of accumulated grievances. Each one becomes magnified by all the other little unforgiven grievances from the past: the microgrievances that seemed too small at the time to make any real effort to forgive. What could have been dispensed with easily now rears up as a monstrous affront. A tiny gust of unforgiveness blows up into a hurricane of recrimination.

Your Ego Is Right (Always)

One way to recognize these backed-up microgrievances in your relationships is by paying attention to language. Do you find yourself saying or thinking things like "She never _____" or "He always _____"? *Never* and *always* are amplifiers. They increase the intensity of the microgrievance by isolating it from whatever small incident happened to set it off and elevating it to a matter of principle that your partner has violated repeatedly. It's no longer about that dirty plate they left sitting by the couch all day; it's about how inconsiderate they are to have left it there and how obtuse not to have noticed your smoldering displeasure over it. The specific becomes generalized: an innocent lapse turns into an intentional affront and a sign of your partner's character defects. It escalates into a matter of right and wrong: you're right and they're wrong.

The moment we decide that we're right and the other is wrong, forgiveness goes out the window. It no longer feels justified. The other person is clearly at fault; it's up to them to admit it and promise to do better next time. Of course they don't see it that way. They counter that your snap judgments and criticism are the real problem. Why can't you let anything go? This leads to a standoff that can go on for years, with each microgrievance adding further weight to your mutual convictions that you are the one who's *right* and they are *wrong*.

Is there any way out of this bind? Not if being right is more important than forgiving. Right and wrong constitute a zero-sum game. If you are right, the other is automatically wrong. Here we see the ego's fragility and its penchant for attack in full glory. The ego must always be right. To admit its flaws would prove too shameful; they would testify to its inferiority. Using attack-other, the ego props up its own image by insisting the other is flawed and trying to make them feel guilty. It diverts us from having to take responsibility for our own behavior, face our own guilt, and forgive it.

A Course in Miracles asks (in a somewhat different context), "*Do you prefer that you be right or happy?*"[3] This too is a zero-sum game. If you insist on being right, you forfeit any chance of being happy. On the other hand, if happiness is your goal, then you cannot be right. Nor can you be wrong. Those categories belong to the ego's world. If happiness is your goal, they no longer apply.

As opposites, right and wrong are polarizing; they cannot be shared. As a result, they increase our sense of separation. We are not joined together in a common purpose. We do not seek the same goal of happiness. We stand on opposite sides, competing to see who's right.

You cannot be right without relying on the past. You elevate your own experience over that of anyone else and, more importantly, over the guidance of the Holy Spirit. Your past may make you right in your own eyes, but it keeps you bound to a vision of your partner as someone different and "other." This blocks forgiveness. As with my grandmother, Minnie, the casualty is happiness.

Happiness can thrive only in the present, where judgment is impossible. The present frees you from the chains of right and wrong. The choice for happiness, then, is also the choice to let go of the past in favor of the present. That is the choice to forgive.

With this understanding, let's take another look at the classic Bible story of Adam and Eve and their expulsion from Eden in order to interpret it in a new light. They ate the fruit of the Tree of Knowledge of Good and Evil. In other words, Adam and Eve, the first humans, lost their knowledge of Oneness and Love and fell into duality. Good and evil, right and wrong—these are judgments made by *us*, not by God or the Holy Spirit. Such judgments split us apart, while He sees us all as equals and equally worthy of love. Only in our "fallen" separated state do concepts like good and evil or right and wrong have any meaning.

The desire to be right leads to arrogance and pride. It justifies attack on those who disagree with you and therefore are wrong. Being wrong leads to guilt and shame. It justifies hiding and defensiveness and, of course, counter-attack. Neither leads to happiness. Happiness has no place in this pernicious equation.

Unlike right and wrong, happiness *can* and *must* be shared. That is its natural condition. No one hoards true happiness and tries to keep it all to themselves, because it would rapidly diminish and disappear. Happiness *wants* to expand. It must radiate outward. It expresses itself through our smile, the bounce in our step, the softness and kindness of our words. Happiness is generous. It gives itself away in the certainty that it is not diminished in the least by sharing. It grows stronger.

The first step in moving beyond the ego's false dichotomy of right and wrong is to decide that in all circumstances happiness is your only goal. As we saw earlier, this means deciding against your own judgments in favor of the Holy Spirit's. Making this one simple decision in your own mind can open the door to miracles, as we saw with Bill Thetford and Arthur and with Judy Whitson and her cousins.

*   *   *

If you and your level-three partner are both students of *A Course in Miracles*, there is another powerful tool at your disposal. Whenever you disagree and you each believe you are right, you can choose to ask the Holy Spirit for guidance *together*. How does this work? You each set aside everything you thought you knew about the problem and how to solve it. More importantly, you release all the judgments that you imposed on your partner. You remind yourself that you don't really know much about anything, but that there is a Presence within both you and your partner that does know and that will gladly share Its wisdom if you ask.

Then sit together with your partner and frame the problem you are having in this way:

In order to be truly helpful, in this situation involving _____, what do I need to know?

What would You have me do?

What would You have us *do?*

Then close your eyes, quiet your mind, and simply listen. (If you've been practicing the Workbook lessons, you will be familiar with this process.) Turn the situation over to the Holy Spirit for help. You want His guidance, not your ego's, and you welcome it even if it seems to go against what you thought was right. When you feel you've received an answer, ask if there's anything more you should know. Then open your eyes, wait for your partner if necessary, and share what you've each learned.

This is a practice we have used at the Foundation for Inner Peace since its inception to request guidance for any major decision, especially if our opinions seem to differ. It works. The answers we receive are rarely identical; rather, they're complementary. Each person gets an important piece of the solution in the form best suited to them. Some see images; others hear words. The guidance combines to form a picture more complete than any one individual would have been capable of.

By asking together, with wholly open minds, we join under the banner of a common cause: truth, peace, happiness. That's our real goal, the outcome we seek together. The specifics don't matter. This process transcends categories of right and wrong. It lifts us out of our separate ego identifications and unites us at the level of mind and spirit, which is our true reality. At this level, all of our seeming problems have been answered already. Miracles follow naturally.

Apology and Forgiveness

Once you understand forgiveness as a choice between "right" and "happy," the decision to forgive becomes easier. To forgive is to give up on right or wrong in favor of happiness. How might this play out in your level-three relationships, where the microgrievances are prone to pile up in a seemingly endless cycle of accusation and recrimination? The moment you realize you're feeling some negative emotion—anything other than peace—you can stop what you're doing, identify where you preferred to be right, and let it go. Forgive it. Metaphorically speaking, you would need to install the happiness app on your mental smartphone to send you an alert when you stray off course into a grievance and redirect you toward happiness. You'd need to make happiness the magnetic north of your emotional compass and move toward it as consistently as possible.

Even if you manage this, however, there's still a problem. How will your partner know that you've jettisoned your need to be right in favor of being happy? If, in the midst of a disagreement, you abruptly paused and broke out in a big smile, it might not be taken well. Your partner might feel belittled or think you're being insincere. They may try to pull you off your pedestal of happiness and forgiveness rather than join you there. In a word, *they* may still prefer to be right, even if *you* do not. Your attempts to convince them that you've found a better way may be heard as a judgment. You need some way to let them know that for you the battle is over, that you've dropped your sword of righteousness and prefer to forgive instead. You're willing to hit the reset and start over with the goal of mutual happiness.

There is a tool for achieving this result. It's not some esoteric mystical incantation. It's something everyone knows, but few make use of. It's called an *apology*. Apologies are widely misunderstood, because we view them as the ego does. To apologize is to admit that you were wrong. Being wrong is shameful. It's a surrender to your opponent and a sign of weakness. It's also an acknowledgment of guilt. No one wants to feel guilty, so naturally they resist apologizing.

How many of us as children were forced to apologize when we knew we hadn't done anything wrong? Or maybe we had, but there was no way we were going to fess up to it. Our early experience with apologies is not very positive, so apologies are now associated with shame. Given this, who would willingly apologize?

If we're stuck playing the ego's right-or-wrong game—if those represent our only choices— then of course we prefer to be right. But if we take the broader view, what *A Course in Miracles* describes as rising "above the battleground,"[4] and from that higher perspective recognize that the real choice is not between right or wrong but right or happy, then an apology becomes something very different. It is a flag of peace, not surrender. It is a punctuation mark: a period lovingly placed at the end of a long and tumultuous sentence. It is not capitulation, not an admission of guilt or wrongdoing, and not a badge of shame. It's a signal to your partner that you prefer peace over conflict, a sign that the storm has passed, the battle over, and it's safe to lay down arms and come together again in peace. Grievances separate; apology unifies.

To be clear, genuine apology does not involve the defense mechanism of *attack-self* (from chapter 5). You are not making yourself wrong and attacking yourself in some exaggerated way in order to spare yourself shame and further attack. To say, "You're right, I'm a terrible person, and I apologize for messing up your life" is not helpful. Nor should an apology be used as a sacrificial gesture in which you, as the more spiritually advanced one, climb up on your cross in order to demonstrate to the other just how guilty (and *wrong*) they really are. These are not examples of forgiveness. They are covert attacks. To attack, no matter the form, can only inflame conflict.

Unfortunately, some seem incapable of apologizing. They will always prefer to be right over being happy and to make the other person wrong. I have seen this tendency play out even among dedicated Course students. Instead of simply saying, "I'm sorry" for slipping into an ego judgment, they deflect the blame onto the person who was hurt. They'll employ phrases like "Well, that's *your* projection, not mine" or "If you think *I'm* attacking *you,* then you're the one making a judgment about me, and that's your problem, not mine." They seem to thrive on projection and attack, with no insight into what they're doing or its consequences.

We could say that their shame is so great that they have made a life choice never to face it under any circumstances. Rather than criticizing them for this and shaming them further, we can acknowledge the times when we've exhibited the same egoic behavior and choose to forgive them, as we ourselves would want to be forgiven. Apply the teaching from Workbook lesson 134, which asks, "*Would I accuse myself of doing this?*"[5] Or, in the wise words of Jesus in the Gospels, "Why do you see the speck in your neighbor's eye, but do not notice the log in your own eye?" (Matthew 7:3, New Revised Standard Version).

You must always attend to your own grievances first. Forgiveness is a process of *inner* healing. It's not about what's happening out there in the world, because that's all projection and illusion. It's about your mind. Once you attend to your own judgments, you're in a better position to respond to someone else's intransigence. Maybe *you* apologize instead. Or maybe you offer a silent blessing and lovingly place them in the Holy Spirit's care. This is another example of that oft-repeated advice to *put on your own oxygen mask first*. You must be grounded in truth before you can help anyone else.

"But why are they like that?" you might ask. "Why do they keep trying to fight with me?" The honest answer is, there's no way to know, and it's not up to you to figure it out. From the Holy Spirit's perspective, any attempt to explain, rationalize, justify, excuse, or interpret another's behavior constitutes a judgment. We spin another story line and assign everyone roles, but they're all equally unreal and therefore equally unworthy of our attempts to make sense of them. The ego is insane; it defies rational understanding. That's true for you, your partner, and everyone else. When you try to understand it or its actions, you are really trying to justify it and make it real. And that will never succeed.

It is not necessary to understand the reasons behind a particular behavior in order to forgive it. In fact, the Course tells us that "*all things must be first forgiven, and then understood.*"[6] True understanding will remain beyond our reach as long as we remain in the ego's hall of mirrors. The projections are too thick and too confusing. Unless we recognize our brothers and sisters for what they are in reality—pieces of the one Self we all share—they will remain incomprehensible to us.

Of course, it is hardly necessary to apologize for every misunderstanding or disagreement. These are so much a part of the ego's world that we would find ourselves apologizing nonstop. But it *is* necessary to *forgive*—at all times, in all circumstances, and in every possible moment.

Your level-three partners are your forgiveness companions. They are guaranteed to provide you with a continual stream of forgiveness opportunities, and that's as it should be. They are your primary teachers, the ones assigned to you as ideal learning partners by the Holy Spirit. It's their job to expose all of the places in you where the ego has burrowed in deep—places you could never have identified on your own. Is it any wonder that they trigger you?

Your ego, however, is not fond of this outing process. It will resist, and you'll find yourself repeating the same forgiveness lessons many times. Please don't beat yourself up over this. (That's what the ego wants!) Accept it and, if possible, appreciate the exquisite learning arrangement you've been given.

In any relationship where something comes up that threatens your sense of peace, the Course advises thus: "*Whoever is saner at the time the threat is perceived should remember how deep is his indebtedness to the other and how much gratitude is due him, and be glad he can pay his debt by bringing happiness to both.*"[7] By choosing forgiveness, we also make the choice for happiness.

When someone triggers me, I like to joke that I've just spotted an "AFO." This is not some new variety of UFO. It is, as many in the Course community like to say, "another forgiveness opportunity." When an AFO appears, please *do* call for help, but not from the Air Force. Call upon the Holy Spirit to help you use the opportunity by forgiving.

Seen in this light, the proper response to our partners is infinite gratitude. We are grateful, because they have given us yet another chance to heal ourselves and fulfill our role in the plan of Atonement and *tikkun olam*. Over time, as you and your partner become better and better learners in the Holy Spirit's curriculum, a lovely change takes place. Those triggers grow less frequent. When they show up, you recognize them for what they are more rapidly and choose forgiveness over the stubborn need to be right. The result? Your relationship becomes more loving. You witness this as it happens; you *feel* it. This gives you the confidence to practice forgiving with ever more determination and consistency. Better still, it leaves you feeling happier!

You and your partner walk the path to God together. You cannot progress without them, and they cannot advance without you. But together, joined in the common purpose of forgiveness, you will awaken to your shared oneness.

Part Three
One Love

⌒

*You cannot enter into real relationships
with any of God's Sons unless you love
them all and equally. Love is not special.
If you single out one part of the Sonship
for your love, you are imposing guilt on
all your relationships and making them
unreal. You can love only as God loves.*[1]

*Forgiveness is the healing of the
perception of separation. . . . Perception
is based on a separated state, so that
anyone who perceives at all needs healing.*[2]

17

To Love Everyone

In chapter 9, we looked at the Jewish mystical doctrine of *tikkun olam*, in which it becomes the task of each human being to help repair God's fractured creation. In theory, this would mean that everyone should join in love with everyone else on the planet in order to knit together what the separation broke. In practice, however, this feels overwhelming. How do we reach out and touch billions with love? It doesn't seem possible.

Over a lifetime, each of us may encounter tens of thousands of people in various capacities. The majority of those encounters will be brief and fleeting. They will be level-one relationships. Our level-two relationships will be far fewer, and our level-threes can be counted on the fingers of our hands—maybe just one hand. How then do we heal the myriad fractured pieces of God's one Son? How do we go from "loving one"—that is, loving one individual, one relationship at a time—to "one love," which embraces everyone everywhere without distinction or judgment? Understood correctly, this is the task we are charged with. This is what both *A Course in Miracles* and *tikkun olam* ask of us.

There are two fundamental approaches we can take. I like to call them "bottom-up" and "top-down" forgiveness.

Bottom-up forgiveness is the more familiar of the two. It's the topic of this book. It starts from within the dream and does not challenge that dream, at least not initially. We clean house; we dust off the accumulated residue of judgments old and new; we tend our garden by uprooting the weeds of grievance wherever they sprout. We apply forgiveness whenever the need shows up in our own lives, in particular to those individuals who seem to threaten or challenge us and to those we've decided to make special. We do our job and trust that others will do theirs. If we all take responsibility for cleaning up our own messy little corner of the relational world, then in the fullness of time all relationships will be healed and the Son of God will be returned to oneness.

Top-down forgiveness proceeds from the opposite direction. It does not register relationships as arrangements between two separate individuals. It starts from the Holy Spirit's vision of what we are and where we are. We cultivate the ability to see with His eyes such that when we encounter our sisters and brothers, we perceive no differences, no bodies, no personalities, only holiness, light, and love. In that light, we recognize our oneness with them, and that is forgiveness. The split mind of God's one Son is mended.

Top-down forgiveness goes well beyond relationships. It envelops the entire world of perception in its light and peace. The five senses still show us differences, but we no longer credit them. They are empty, transparent. With the vision of Christ and the Holy Spirit, we see through them to the light within. The ego's illusions lose their power to deceive, because we recognize them for what they are. They are nothing.

Top-down would seem to be the more comprehensive approach, because it is not limited to any single relationship. It transforms them all simultaneously. It is the path that we all come to in the end, because it leads to the lovely experience the Course calls "the real world," which in turn leads directly back to God. But for most, top-down is not an option. The profound shift in perception that it requires is too unsettling without years of committed spiritual practice. Until you begin to perceive the oneness in all things, it will remain a distant goal.

Bottom-up Forgiveness

Bottom-up forgiveness proceeds relationship by relationship. Even though we understand that we will reach only a tiny fraction of the separated Sons of God, we're content to work with what we're given. We focus on each relationship very specifically, because our grievances are specific. It's that one difficult person who sets us off as only they can. "*Hate is specific.*"[1] The need to forgive is specific as well, and is targeted to those particular relationships. Although forgiveness is the means by which the Atonement progresses and therefore applies to the entire world of separation, to the extent that we need to forgive specifically, forgiveness will appear to be specific.

> *Complete abstraction is the natural condition of the mind. But part of it is now unnatural. It does not look on everything as one. It sees instead but fragments of the whole, for only thus could it invent the partial world you see. . . .*
>
> *Thus were specifics made. And now it is specifics we must use in practicing. We give them to the Holy Spirit, that He may employ them for a purpose which is different from the one we gave to them.*[2]

If we set out to repair the fractured Son of God one relationship at a time, it doesn't take much imagination to realize that, even if everyone plays their part perfectly, the repair will take a very long time to reach completion. That would indeed be true if people really were separate and time progressed in a linear fashion, minute by minute, day after day, year upon year. However, that is not the Course's view of time. It looks on time from the perspective of eternity, where all of time has already been and gone. In truth, it never happened at all. It's part of the ego's illusion: its big con game. And so there is another way of understanding bottom-up forgiveness that lifts it beyond specifics and frees it from the chains of time.

Within the dream of separation, we appear to be distinct and unique, but in truth we remain exactly as God created us: not separate, but joined; not bodies, but spirit. Because we were created as one, that oneness remains alive within each of us, even though we're no longer aware of it. Although people appear to be separate and specific, they are also simultaneously that oneness. "*One brother is all brothers. Every mind contains all minds, for every mind is one.*"[3] The part contains the whole. In fact, the part *is* the whole, because in Oneness *there can be no parts.* Therefore, heal any of the parts and you *are* healing the whole. Healing is not selective; it is holographic.

Forgive one specific individual, and your forgiveness must extend to all others, because they are one with you. "*Forgiveness cannot be for one and not the other.*"[4] The healing of one relationship ripples outward to catalyze the healing of others. This healing can be received by any part that is willing to accept it. Not all of them are. Most have their shields raised against it, because they've identified with ego and perceive love as a threat. At some deep level, however, they cannot help but feel it. "*The light in one awakens it in all. And when you see it in your brother, you* are *remembering for everyone.*"[5] In this sense, Love awakens the realization of its own eternal presence.

The Nexus of Love

It's easy to become discouraged about the state of the world and question whether it's really worthwhile to practice forgiveness and carry on the work of the Atonement. Tune into the nightly news, and all you'll hear is conflict: political clashes, natural disasters, economic threats, mass shootings. How can your own small efforts at forgiveness remedy problems on that scale?

The ego would have us focus on everything that's wrong in the world. It encourages us to make judgments—the more inflexible, the better—which it uses to foment grievances and hatred. The ego wants us to see our sisters and brothers as sinful. How can people be so greedy, so cruel, so ignorant, we ask? The ego relishes such questions, because they cannot be satisfactorily answered within the ego's framework. Without those answers, we grow fearful. But there is an untold story here that seldom makes the nightly news. It is a story about how much love there really is in the world.

Our love is imperfect; there's no doubting that. It is splintered and confined to specific relationships, just as we are. It is but the dimmest, most distorted reflection of love as God knows Love to be. Nonetheless, however faint and feeble it may be, it is still love. It cannot be vanquished, disguised, or suppressed despite the ego's unceasing efforts. And we recognize love's presence the instant we feel it.

Love is the essence of God. God is Love and Love is God—most will agree about that. Nothing in the ego's world is capable of eradicating love, because, as we've said many times, *illusions cannot overcome truth*. The ego can never triumph over God. Love is therefore invulnerable and invincible.

Nevertheless, to experience love, to feel it, we must want it and choose it. We do this by giving it. When we give love, we affirm our lineage from God. We remember, however faintly, the truth of what we are.

Every loving thought that the Son of God ever had is eternal. The loving thoughts his mind perceives in this world are

the world's only reality. They are still perceptions, because he
still believes that he is separate. Yet they are eternal because
they are loving. And being loving, they are like the Father,
and therefore cannot die.[6]

Let's consider for a moment how much love we all share already. We are born with love for our parents. That love can be scuttled when parents are abusive or neglectful, but it remains the default setting. Young men dying on the battlefield cry out not for God or country, but for their mothers. On the flip side, there is the love parents feel for their children. There is the love of siblings for each other, the love shared by close friends over the course of a lifetime, the unspoken love of those who've come through tough times together or labored toward a common goal, the love between life partners who grow closer with each passing year. We could go on. Yes, the specific form taken by each relationship is unique, but the love within it is not. It does not change from one relationship to the next. Like water poured into vessels of different shape, it remains the same. It will quench your thirst. Love is always love.

Imagine for a moment all of this love generated by the billions upon billions of relationships on planet earth. Picture each expression of love as a ray of light connecting two or more people, or as a luminous string linking them together. Now think how many of these rays or strings extend out from each person on earth over the course of a lifetime.

If you visualize all of earth's inhabitants interconnected in this way, they form a powerful nexus of love and light. It becomes impossible to single out any individual ray or strand of love, because there are far too many, and they all run together and shine with equal brightness. The love we feel for each other—love that's expressed through specific, one-to-one relationships—joins us all. When you view this nexus of love in its entirety, what do you see? Only light, only love. It is like a magnificent star blazing in perfect radiance. Picturing this, you begin to get the faintest idea of the love God has for us all. And that Love is what we are. It is our inheritance and our identity.

When you see in your brothers and sisters, not the shell of the relationship, but only this light, this love that dwells within all, then forgiveness will have served its purpose. Their bodies, their life stories, their personal dramas—all will fade into this light; all will melt into this love. Your forgiveness transforms the darkened world that arose from the separation and returns it to the light of love. That light dispels the ego, its judgments, its grievances, and its specialness. They are like thin tendrils of fog that emerged from the shadows to enfold you—taking on form to become substantial, invested with meaning, both alluring and frightening. But when the light grows sufficiently bright, the fog retreats and the shadows dissolve back into nothingness.

This is forgiveness's endgame. This is the "real world" that the Course so often mentions. Although it is still part of the dream of separation, it poses no further obstacles to love and the full return of God and oneness. It is "real" because truth now shines through it.

Illusion makes illusion. Except one. Forgiveness is illusion that is answer to the rest.

Forgiveness sweeps all other dreams away, and though it is itself a dream, it breeds no others. All illusions save this one must multiply a thousandfold. But this is where illusions end. Forgiveness is the end of dreams, because it is a dream of waking. It is not itself the truth. Yet does it point to where the truth must be, and gives direction with the certainty of God Himself. It is a dream in which the Son of God awakens to His Self and to his Father, knowing They are one.[7]

If we do the work of bottom-up forgiveness, progressing relationship by relationship; if we apply the Holy Spirit's ultimate reframe to all our grievances as soon as they arise, forgiveness moves inevitably toward oneness. The specific slips quietly into the abstract and "one brother" indeed becomes "all brothers."

As we progress, we will find that we no longer relate to specific individuals and their ego-based identities. Our only relationship is with the Son of God as He appears in each seemingly separate person. Differences we once found jarring are barely noticed and not in the least disturbing. Should they grab our attention, it's only for the purpose of healing. Light, love, and peace increasingly become our reality. They are what we seek and find in all our sisters and brothers.

At this point, bottom-up and top-down forgiveness join hands and merge. One relationship is all relationships, and their sole purpose is forgiveness.

When the Holy Spirit has at last led you to Christ . . . perception fuses into knowledge because perception has become so holy that its transfer to holiness is merely its natural exten-sion. Love transfers to love without any interference, for the two are one. As you perceive more and more common ele-ments in all situations, the transfer of training under the Holy Spirit's guidance increases and becomes generalized. Gradually you learn to apply it to everyone and everything, for its applicability is universal. When this has been accom-plished, perception and knowledge have become so similar that they share the unification of the laws of God.

What is one cannot be perceived as separate, and the denial of the separation is the reinstatement of knowledge. At the altar of God, the holy perception of God's Son becomes so enlightened that light streams into it. . . . The world has no purpose as it blends into the purpose of God. For the real world has slipped quietly into Heaven, where everything eternal in it has always been.[8]

Love has returned to love. And with that we say, "Amen."

About This Series

This book is the second in a series of five books devoted to bringing the principles of *A Course in Miracles* to the general reader while offering the experienced student a deeper understanding of its insights. The first book was *From Never-Mind to Ever-Mind: Transforming the Self to Embrace Miracles*. Book 3 will be titled *From Fear to Eternity: The Journey of A Course in Miracles*. It will delve more deeply into specific Course topics like the nature of time, the body, sickness and healing, death, the real world, and the holy instant. Book 4 will use a Q&A format to discuss common misunderstandings about the Course and controversial topics like the role of sex and money in the life of the Course student. Book 5 will offer something entirely different: a summary of all that came before, and yet also a completely new approach to the Course's central teaching that *nothing real can be threatened. Nothing unreal exists. Herein lies the peace of God.*

Acknowledgments

I would like to thank Dan Strutzel for approaching me with this writing assignment from Spirit and for shepherding the process along. Thanks as well to Gilles Dana, Ellen Goldberg, Evan Litzenblatt, and the rest of the G&D team for their commitment to this series.

I am immensely grateful to my editor, Richard Smoley, whom I have admired since his *Gnosis* magazine days. Thank you, Richard, for knowing just where to apply your fine editorial touch to make my prose emerge clean and taut. It's an honor to work together.

I would also like to acknowledge and thank Vic Kelly, MD, and Donald Nathanson, MD, for opening my eyes to the unique contribution of Silvan Tomkins, PhD, in understanding the hows and whys of emotion, in particular the hidden emotion of shame.

And finally, I must thank the many individuals and couples I have worked with in psychotherapy over the years. You trusted me with your innermost secret shames and fears. This book could not have come about without you.

Notes

Direct quotations from *A Course in Miracles* are in italics; all emphasis is from the original. The notes use the standard reference numbering of *A Course in Miracles* as published by the Foundation for Inner Peace. This enables students to refer to a specific passage within the Course and its supplements. References are to the combined third edition. For convenience, page numbers have been added.

The key to the references is as follows:

T stands for the Text. **W** stands for the Workbook. **M** stands for the Manual for Teachers. **C** stands for Clarification of Terms (at the end of the Manual). **P** stands for *Psychotherapy: Purpose, Process, and Practice.* **S** stands for *The Song of Prayer.*

Here is an example:

> *"You will first dream of peace, and then awaken to it"*
> (T-13.VII.9:1).

T = Text

13 = chapter 13

VII = section VII (of chapter 13)

9 = paragraph 9 (in section VII)

1 = line 1 (of paragraph 9)

Another example:

> *"We say 'God is,' and then we cease to speak, for in that knowledge words are meaningless"* (W-pI.169.5:4).

W = Workbook

pI = part I (of the Workbook)

169 = lesson 169

5 = paragraph 5

4 = line 4 (of paragraph 5)

Endnotes

Preface

1 *A Course in Miracles*, Text-Intro.1:6–7, p. 1.
2 ACIM, W-pII.229, p. 406.

Part 1

1 T-20.IV.6:5, p. 433.

Chapter 1

1 T-11.III.1:7, p. 199.
2 W-pII.336, p. 470.
3 T-6.II.5:5, p. 97.
4 T-21.Intro.1:5, p. 445.
5 W-pII.304.1:3, p. 451.
6 T-5.II.2:5, p. 75.

Chapter 2

1 W-pI.108, p. 195.

Chapter 3

1   T-16.V.2:3, p. 341.
2   T-12.IV.1:4, p. 223.
3   T-16.IV.7:1–2, pp. 338–39.
4   T-16.V.6:1, p. 342.
5   T-16.V. 7:1–8:3, p. 342.
6   T-16.V. 7:5, p. 342.
7   T-7.I.4:1–4, pp. 112–13.
8   T-22.Intro.2:5–3:5, p. 467.

Chapter 4

1   T-4.II.2:1–2, p. 56.
2   T-13.VII.11:1–6, p. 256.
3   T-17.IV.2:3–4, p. 358.
4   T-13.VII.12:1–6; 13:1–3, pp. 256–57.
5   T-15.VII.8:2, p. 318.
6   W-pI.185.3:3–5, 4:4–5, p. 348.

Chapter 5

1   T-15.IX.2:3, p. 322.
2   T-22.I.4:7–10, p. 469.
3   T-4.I.8:1, pp. 54–55.
4   T-6.V.A.5:9, p. 105.
5   T-9.VIII.3:4, p. 178.
6   T-12.V.1:2–2:5, p. 225.
7   T-1.VI.2:1, p. 14.
8   T-10.II.4:1–5:4, pp. 183–84.

Chapter 6

1   T-15.V.1:1–4, p. 312.
2   T-15.V.9:1–5, pp. 313–14.

3   P-3.II.1:3, p. 19.
4   T-15.V.4:5–6, p. 312.
5   T-15.III.12:1–4, p. 309.
6   T-12.IV.1:4, p. 223.
7   W-pI.79.1:1–3; 2:1–2; 6:2, p. 141.
8   T-17.III.6:1–4, p. 356.
9   T-15.IV.9:7, p. 311.
10 T-14.VII.6:1–11, p. 288.
11 T-14.VI.2:1–4, p. 285.
12 T-20.VI.2:5–7, p. 436.
13 T-12.VII.8:1, p. 231.
14 T-10.I.2:1–6, p. 182.

Chapter 7

1   Elaine Pagels, *The Gnostic Gospels* (New York, Vintage, 1979), pp. xix–xx.
2   Pagels, *Gnostic Gospels*, p. 152.
3   T-14.VI.1:4, p. 285.
4   T-11.VIII.13:1–3, p. 214.
5   T-12.II.4:2–5:3, p. 219.
6   T-Intro.1:7, p. 1.
7   T-11.III.5:1–2, p. 199.
8   W-pI.94, 110, and 162 (titles), pp. 164, 199, 307.
9   T-13.IX.8:1–2, 6–7, 13, p. 262.
10 W-pI.69.4:2–5:4, p. 117.
11 T-13.X.9:4–6, p. 264.
12 T-12.VII.9:1, p. 231.
13 T-31.VIII.3:2, p. 666.

Part II

1   W-pI.62.1:1, 4–5, p. 104.

Chapter 8

1   T-preface, p. xii.

2   T-17.V.2:1-2, p. 362

3   W-pI.185.12:4–5, p. 350.

4   T-14.X.12:5, p. 296.

5   W-pII.288.1:2–4, p. 441.

6   T-14.X.10:1, 7, p. 295.

7   P-2.In.4:3, p. 4.

8   P-3.II.4:6–7, p. 20.

9   T-20.VI.5:1, p. 437.

10   T-15.V.4:6, p. 312.

11   T-20.VI.8:1-6, pp. 437–38.

12   T-12.II.2:7, p. 218.

13   T-8.III.6:1–2, p. 143.

Chapter 9

1   T-13.VI.13:1, p. 253.

2   T-3.II.1:8, p. 38.

3   T-2.VII.6:1-5, 9, p. 33.

4   T-18.I.4:1–4; 5:6, pp. 372–73.

5   T-28.III.7:4–5, p. 597.

6   T-18.VII.5:5, p. 389.

7   T-21.In.1:7–8, p. 445.

8   T-1.I.25:1–2, p. 4.

9   T-1.III.3:1–4, p. 9.

10   T-6.II.1:5, p. 96.

11   T-7.VI.7:7, p. 125.

12   T-21.II.9:5–6, p. 450.

13   T-12.VII.8:1, p. 231.

14   T-14.V.11:6, p. 284.

15   T-18.II.6:4–7:2, p. 377.

16   T-20.V.1:1–8, p. 434.

Chapter 10

1   W-pI.216.1:2–4, p. 395.

2   W-pI.72.2:1, p. 124.

3   W-pI.71.1:1–2, 2:1–5, p. 121.

4   W-pI.68.1:1–6, 2:1–5, p. 115.

Chapter 11

1   W-pII.1.2:1–2; 3:1–3, p. 401.

2   Lenore Terr, MD, *Too Scared to Cry* (New York: Basic Books, 1990), pp. 127–29.

3   W-pII.289, p. 442.

4   T-13.VI.2:1–3; 3:5–7, pp. 250–51.

5   W-pII.1.1:1–6, p. 401.

6   W-pII.1.1:1, p. 401

7   T-Intro.2:2–4, p. 1.

8   T-27.II.10:1, p. 570.

9   T-16.I.3:12, p. 331.

10   T-17.III.1:1–3, p. 354.

11   T-12.II.1:5, p. 218.

12   T-2.II.1:11–2:3, p. 19.

13   T-17.III.8:2, p. 357.

Chapter 12

1   Stanislav Grof, *When the Impossible Happens: Adventures in Non-Ordinary Realities* (Boulder, Colo.: Sounds True, 2006), pp. 92–94.

2   T-26.IX.3:1–2; 6:1–6, pp. 561–62.

Chapter 13

1   T-19.IV.C.i.11:8-10, p. 419

2   W-pI.197.4:1–2, p. 377.

3   W-pII.1.1:1–4, p. 401.

4   W-pII.289.1:6, p. 442.

Chapter 14

1   T-17.IV.7:1–3. p. 359.

2   T-6.II.3:5–8, p. 96.

3   T-6.II.5:1–3, p. 97.

4   William Shakespeare, *The Tempest*, act 5, scene 1, line 275.

5   T-16.VI.8:1, p. 346.

6   T-7.II.3:3, p. 114.

7   T-7.VII.3:9–10, p. 127.

8   S-2.I.4:2–6, p. 10.

9   T-8.III.4:1–5, p. 142.

10   T-5.III.1:1; 3:4–5, p. 78.

11   T-9.V.8:4, p. 172.

12   T-12.I.3:3–4, p. 215.

13   T-12.I.6:1–2, p. 216.

14   T-6.I.13:2, p. 94.

Chapter 15

1   T-2.V.18:2–6, p. 28.

2   P-3.II.1:3, p. 19.

3   W-pI.158.4:1, p. 298.

4   W-pI.78.10:1–3, p. 140.

5   T-17.III.8:2, p. 357.

6   W-pII.1.1:1, p. 401.

7   T-31.I.12:1–13:5, p. 648.

Chapter 16

1   M-3.5:2, p. 8.
2   T-23.IV.1:10–12, p. 496.
3   T-29.VII.1:9, p. 617.
4   T-23.IV (see especially 5:1–7), pp. 496–497.
5   W-pI.134.9:3, p. 249.
6   T-30.V.1:6. p. 635.
7   T-18.V.7:1, p. 384.

Part III

1   T-13.X.11:1–4, p. 265.
2   T-3.V.9:1, 10:3, p. 46.

Chapter 17

1   W-pI.161.7:1, p. 305.
2   W-pI.161.2:1–4; 3:1-3, p. 304.
3   W-pI.161.4:1–2, p. 304.
4   T-27.II.3:9, p. 569.
5   T-21.I.10:6–7, p. 447.
6   T-11.VII.2:1–5, p. 210.
7   W-pI.198.2:8 to 3:7, p. 379.
8   T-12.VI.6:3–7; 7:1–5, p. 229.